LIVING OUR VALUES

An 'inside-out' approach to change your world for the better

Praise for *Living Our Values*

This is an outstanding book which I believe would be helpful for everybody. The values are explored very clearly and can provide a terrific blueprint for life. This is a very practical read with many suggestions about ways to look into one's self and one's life alone and with others. For those who are 'spiritual seekers' the book is highly relevant but equally so for those of us that may be somewhat put off by the word 'spiritual'. I wholeheartedly encourage you to absorb this important book and I believe it will make a difference in all aspects of your work and personal lives.

Graham Alexander, founder of the Alexander Corporation and author of *Super Coaching* and *Tales from the Top*

This book is an excellent tool for spiritual and personal development. It elucidates 12 higher values to encourage practice and help you be the change! The book is easy to read and apply with useful points for reflection. As a spiritual coach myself, I found the book very uplifting and as it so gracefully reminds us, 'the time is now!'

Caroline Shola Arewa, author of *Opening to Spirit*, personal development coach, speaker

The last decade has seen humanity being conned into believing that material goods are the measure of true worth. The current crisis of liberal capitalism has exposed this confidence trick, and now this thought-provoking book brings us back to the path of rediscovering the true values which guide homo sapiens. We have been 'clever' but not 'wise' and now the values expressed here, and the exercises we are invited to explore, bring our souls back into a true orientation to the common good – valuing our true selves and our human kin.

Professor Peter Gilbert, Emeritus Professor of Social Work and Spirituality at Staffordshire University

Once again the spiritual wisdom and the clarity of the teaching of the Brahma Kumaris comes alive on the page. In a fast moving world this guide provides a deep and meaningful exploration into the heart of Values. The exercises are easy to follow and will be of meaning and value in a range of settings. The work of the Brahma Kumaris is transforming the world we live in.

Jackee Holder, author, coach, coach trainer and intuitive facilitator

Living Our Values is a truly valuable and essential book for this time. It recognises and expresses so well the issues that humanity is facing today and, of course, does not shy or shrink from the key spiritual life of which we are a part. That is perhaps the only way we can rediscover our values – something that communists and capitalists have lost. This book balances the material and the spiritual beautifully. Brahma Kumaris and Dadi Janki in particular can so well show us the way of life.

Sir John Whitmore, Director of Performance Consultants International and author of *Coaching For Performance*

I have always admired the Brahma Kumari's commitment to service and to making spiritual information free to those who need it across the planet. This book is another valuable and practical contribution to raising consciousness and spreading love.

Nick Williams, author of eight books, including *The Work We Were Born To Do*, and co-founder of Inspired Entrepreneur

LIVING OUR VALUES

An 'inside-out' approach to change your world for the better

BRAHMA KUMARIS

LIVING OUR VALUES

Brahma Kumaris

www.bkpublications.com
email: enquiries@bkpublications.com
www.bkwsu.org

First edition of this book was created to honour
the 50th anniversary of the United Nations in 1995

Second edition edited by John McConnel

PRINT ISBN: 978-1-886872-63-9
KINDLE ISBN: 978-1-886872-64-6
E-PUB ISBN: 978-1-886872-65-3

Published by Brahma Kumaris Information Services Ltd. in
association with Brahma Kumaris World Spiritual University (UK)

Registered Charity No. 269971

Global Co-operation House,
65–69 Pound Lane, London NW10, 2HH UK

Designed and typeset by Makar Publishing Production, Edinburgh
Printed by CPI Group (UK) Ltd., Croydon, CR0 4YY

DEDICATION

*For all our global family and everyone
who wants to make the world a better place.*

*Know that you are the creator of your own life
and the hero of your own story.*

This is for you.

Here is everything you would have chosen to remember.

It passes now into your care.

Traveller: The Seven Keys of Enlightenment, Barbara Bossert

Contents

Acknowledgements   xi

Preface *by Dadi Janki*   xiii

Introduction   xv

SECTION 1   EXPLORING OUR VALUES

The Values Statements   2

Co-operation   4

Freedom   7

Happiness   10

Honesty   13

Humility   16

Love   19

Peace   22

Respect   27

Responsibility   31

Simplicity   34

Tolerance   37

Unity   40

SECTION 2   THINK ABOUT IT

Tools for Personal Change and Transformation   44

Remember the Three 'A's   45

Turn Within   47

Contents

Let Your Conscience be Your Guide   48

Pay Attention to Your Intentions   49

Create Quality Thoughts   51

Remember the Law of Action and Reaction   52

Break Negative Thought Patterns   54

Take Time Out   55

Put an End to Wasteful Thinking   56

Remember 'Not' and 'Dot'   57

Don't Ask "Why?", Simply Fly!   58

Generate Pure Thoughts and Good Wishes   59

Develop an Attitude of Gratitude   60

Believe and Achieve   61

Appreciate Rather than Denigrate   62

Have Pure Vision for the Self and Others   63

Influence the Atmosphere   64

Practise Divine Virtues   65

Be Power-Packed and Powerful   66

SECTION 3 MAKING IT HAPPEN

Values Workshops and Activities for Collective Change   69

INDIVIDUALS

Inner Leadership Workshop   71

ORGANISATIONS

Workshop for Professionals   85

COMMUNITIES

Examining Our Current and Future Values   94

Caring for the Environment   103

Fulfilling the Global Vision Workshop   105

FAMILIES

Workshops for Building Family Relationships   108

CLASSROOMS

Sharing Values for a Better World: Curriculum   137

APPENDIX 1 Making the Impossible Possible
                    – the benefits of Raja Yoga meditation   146

APPENDIX 2 10 Ways to Change the World   149

APPENDIX 3 About the Brahma Kumaris   151

APPENDIX 4 Addresses of Brahma Kumaris Centres   152

APPENDIX 5 Further Reading   154

ACKNOWLEDGEMENTS

This book would not have been possible without the input of many people over many years.

It is based on the teachings, insights and research of students and teachers of Raja Yoga meditation as taught by the Brahma Kumaris.

A great debt is owed to the vision and commitment of Brahma Baba, founder of the Brahma Kumaris, who was inspired to set up the organisation in the 1930's in India. His teachings, wisdom and the power of his example infuse this book.

Likewise, tribute must be made to the outstanding women who, as a matter of principle, have led and nurtured the organisation from a community of 300 people to a world-wide spiritual university with over one million students. In particular, we would like to acknowledge the loving administration of the late Dadi Prakashmani, the silent wisdom of Dadi Gulzar and the drive, determination and powerful intellect of Dadi Janki, the current head of the organisation.

Thanks must also be given to the support and vision of Sister Jayanti Kirpalani, Sister Mohini Panjabi and the research undertaken by Gayatri Naraine and Anthony Strano who put much time and effort into creating the first edition of this book, which was created to honour the 50th anniversary of the United Nations in 1995.

Thanks also to the late Lord David Ennals, human rights campaigner and long-time friend of the Brahma Kumaris, for his commitment to peace; Mike George, Ken O'Donnel, Diane Tilman, Rebecca Ortega and Valeriane Bernard who created the workshops; Margaret Barron who wrote the Appendix on meditation; Carol Gill who edited the first edition of the book; and John McConnel, who edited this edition.

PREFACE

by
Dadi Janki
Administrative Head
Brahma Kumaris

We are living in one of the most exciting and challenging times in the history of the world. Everything is changing so fast! Social, economic, political and ecological systems are breaking down and there are many scenes of war, conflict and natural disaster coming in front of us almost every day. Amid the questions, chaos and confusion, there are signs of hope as the human spirit seeks to understand and make sense of it all.

There is now widespread recognition that we have to change our way of living – that materialism, in all its many forms (including science), can no longer provide all the solutions. But what can we do? The answers lie in the hands of each one of us.

There needs to be a radical shift in our consciousness and a return to inner spiritual values.

A life without spiritual values is like being an orphaned child; we feel insecure, unloved and unwanted. Values are our 'parents' – the human soul is nurtured by the values it holds. A sense of security and comfort comes when we know and live our values.

Values are like precious jewels. Lying deep within the soul of each human being, they are the treasure of life. They make us happy, healthy and wealthy.

A life filled with values is a life of self-respect and dignity. The soul is able to come closer to God and life becomes real and meaningful.

Values bring independence and freedom, expand our capacity to be self-sufficient and liberate us from external influences. The soul develops the ability to discern truth and to follow the path of truth.

Values offer protection and anyone who experiences this is able to share this protection with others.

PREFACE

Values bring empowerment and it becomes possible to remove our weaknesses and defects. As the innate goodness of the individual is concentrated on values, the link with God becomes strong and clear. Service is then rendered to others through thoughts, words and actions. A soul with values is not trapped by any limited desires or attractions and remains stable in the unlimited.

Values open the heart and transform human nature so that life is filled with compassion and humility.

As we develop values within the self, we share the fragrance of those values with the world around us and move forward to a better world.

I especially invite you, dear reader, to become part of the solution to the challenges we all face.

You can start by taking part in a powerful experiment using your own inner values.

The experiment has three steps:

1. Go within and cultivate an inner awareness of peace, love, honesty, or any of the other natural values within the soul that appeal to you. Practice this for a few minutes every day. It can be in the morning, the evening, or while you are in action in the world. It can be in the form of prayer, meditation, reflection, or whatever is your own spiritual practice.

2. Notice what experiences begin to emerge from inside you and manifest around you. Make a note in a journal of your experiences each day.

3. Share the story of your daily practice and observations once a week with others. In particular, notice the change in your awareness, attitude, vision and action.

With love and in remembrance of the One.

BK Janki

INTRODUCTION

This book takes you on an exploration of those innermost values that influence our personal attitude, outlook and behaviour. You can journey inside as deeply and honestly as you wish, using each value as a searchlight to discover what lies within the self. Such effort will reward you with more meaningful insights into, and experience of, the higher purpose of your life.

It will also enable you to uncover and recognise your full potential, not only in relation to the self but also the work you do and the community in which you live and serve.

Human dignity is the external expression of an internal state of self-worth. Anyone who really understands their own inherent worth and respects that of others, knows that worth is not something assigned by external sources. It comes from a source that is universal and eternal. This book will help you to touch that source, guiding you towards a more profound understanding of the true nature of the self and others.

The notion of 'self', of course, has been the object of much contemplation and discussion but, at its essence, it is *the dignity and worth of each human being and the sacredness, or divine nature, of human life.*

This book aims to assist the individual and the collective to find the way back to our original divine roots through a process of exploring, learning and making it happen.

Such a process embraces the real meaning and purpose of spiritual and moral education, which is not to impose an ideology or particular set of values on anyone but, rather, to draw out, or to elicit, the best from within the individual.

Values are the underlying motivators of our life. They are of two types: *innate* values (i.e. the intrinsic, original values of the self/soul), and *acquired* values (i.e. the ones we adopt based on the culture of the society in which we happen to live).

Today, many people are largely influenced, and define their true worth, by 'acquired' material values such as social position, monetary worth, external appearance and personal possessions. This misrepresentation of the source of our innate true worth creates cultures of accumulation, possessiveness, selfishness and greed and is the root cause of conflict, exploitation, poverty and world tension.

There is wide recognition of a hierarchy of values, which ascends from the 'lower' material values to 'higher' spiritual values, such as peace, love, care, selflessness and generosity. Such 'higher order' values are universal; they transcend the uniqueness of humanity's richly diverse cultural, philosophical and social heritage. They form a common bedrock on which to build good relationships within and between different communities and nations.

The twelve higher values described in this book – **Co-operation, Freedom, Happiness, Honesty, Humility, Love, Peace, Respect, Responsibility, Simplicity, Tolerance and Unity** – are fundamental to the well-being of humanity as a whole and inspire positive change. The world will automatically become a better place when each of us connects with these inner values and becomes a better person.

Using this Guidebook

Living Our Values contains three main sections; together they offer a process or recipe for creating a better world, which can be summarised as follows:

When we recognise, appreciate and connect with our inner values and consistently apply them in daily life with pure, powerful thoughts and intentions, things will change for the better.

Practice really does make perfect and we *can* make a great difference to the quality of our own life and that of others. With courage, faith and determination, love will ultimately triumph over fear, the positive will overcome the negative and goodness will defeat evil.

Section 1: Exploring Our Values

Each of the twelve values is discussed in both conceptual and practical terms. Readers may want to enjoy a sampling of all these Value Statements in one sitting, then savour each one later as inspirational reading. The Value Statements are deep. Reflecting on one point,

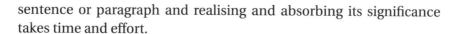

sentence or paragraph and realising and absorbing its significance takes time and effort.

Section 2: Think About It – Tools for Personal Change and Transformation

Focusing on the individual, this section explains some of the premises and concepts in the Value Statements and offers tools and methods to help build spiritual capacity and sustain positive change, including:

○ How to align thoughts, words and actions with universal principles of human conduct;

○ How the consequences of actions are inescapable;

○ How individuals can maintain 'cleanliness' in thoughts, words and deeds;

○ How to gain mastery over thoughts and change wasteful thought patterns;

○ How to have good wishes and pure feelings for others.

Section 3: Making It Happen – Workshops and Activities for Collective Change

This section offers facilitated group sessions designed to help participants identify ways to 'live' their values – at home, at work, at school, in the community and in the world. Activities include dialogues, seminars, creative group sessions and other strength-based approaches.

Background and Context

This book was originally published in 1995 under the title *Living Values – A Guidebook* in honour of the 50th anniversary of the United Nations. It was part of an international initiative called *Sharing Our Values for a Better World* (SVBW) created and co-ordinated by the Brahma Kumaris. (For further information about the Brahma Kumaris see Appendix 3 or visit www.bkwsu.org.)

The aims of the SVBW project were to:

1) Raise awareness of the existence of higher order values as spiritual qualities inherent within the individual regardless of political, economic, cultural, professional, or ethnic background;

Introduction

2) Create a safe and enabling environment for individuals to explore and express these spiritual values, individually and collectively;

3) Offer specific self-development and self-management methods, techniques and group dynamics, which could be used to revive and strengthen spiritual values within the individual;

4) Increase awareness of the value of self-development, both individual and collective, as a contribution to a better quality of life.

The project was very successful and took on a life of its own. It has had considerable impact throughout the world, resulting in a number of 'Living Values' initiatives, especially in the fields of education and health care.

The project itself was the result of another initiative by the Brahma Kumaris called 'Global Co-operation for a Better World' in which the people of many nations were challenged to create their visions of a better world. The findings were analysed and the project leaders came to the conclusion that human beings everywhere want the same things in life, namely a better world in which:

○ All people celebrate the joy of life;

○ Human rights are respected and upheld and the dignity and integrity of all people is assured;

○ People live in ways that preserve nature's ecological balance in an environment that is beautiful and clean;

○ The planet's natural and abundant resources are shared equitably and the basic human needs of all people are provided for;

○ All people have equal opportunities to realise their potential through an educational process that has human, moral and spiritual values at its heart;

○ Life within the immediate family is loving, caring and fulfilling and is the foundation for harmony within the broader human family;

○ There is respect, understanding and tolerance in all human relations;

○ People communicate openly and in a spirit of equality and goodwill;

- Social, economic and political justice is ensured through honesty, responsibility and respect for the rule of law;
- Governments, as representatives of their people, are committed to their well-being. People participate co-operatively in efforts for a secure and peaceful world;
- Science serves humanity and appropriate technology is applied to ensure sustainable development and enhance the quality of life;
- All people enjoy freedom of expression, movement and belief while respecting the liberties and rights of others.

The resulting book, *Visions of a Better World*,[1] containing many uplifting statements and beautiful artistic expressions and poems, was well received and is still being used by thought leaders, educators and culture creatives around the world as a source of inspiration and a powerful reminder of the collective wisdom in the world.

The book did raise one important question, which is still being answered, namely: ***How can we use our collective wisdom to create a better world?***

As we shall see, values in action are the route to change. We can make it happen – one person at a time!

---

1 *Visions of a Better World*, Brahma Kumaris.

SECTION 1

EXPLORING OUR VALUES

I have come to believe that all human beings possess these innate qualities to give love, to care, to grow and to create a sense of belonging for others. Equally, I have come to believe that all human beings have an innate need for love, care, growth and to belong.

Tex Gunning, from the Foreword to *Something Beyond Greatness: Conversations with a Man of Science & a Woman of God*, Judy Rogers and Gayatri Naraine, Health Communications, Inc., 2009

THE VALUES STATEMENTS

These are days when many people are pausing to inquire into intrinsic values and to commit themselves anew to bringing them into their life. For the Brahma Kumaris, values such as peace, purity, wisdom, love and joy are innate in all souls. Seen from this perspective, the desperate search for values is based on a longing for something that we have forgotten but subconsciously remember – our original unconditioned self.

External commitments to values-based processes without internal experience and conviction cannot succeed. All real changes – whether big changes in the world or small changes in a single life – occur as a sequence of subtle shifts, beginning with a change in *awareness*.

A change in awareness precipitates a change in *attitude*. Our attitude colours our *vision*. When we see the world in a new way, we can no longer act the same as before. New actions generate a new world.

So the subtle sequence for all real change is *awareness, attitude, vision, action* and *the world*.

This sequence is values-neutral. It is the same whether we are talking about a move to fear or a move to peace.

An awareness of fear expands to become a fearful attitude. When we have a fearful attitude we see danger everywhere and then take action to protect ourselves, eventually creating an armoured world.

On the other hand, when we have an awareness of peace, our attitude shifts to one of peace, we see everything with peaceful eyes, our peaceful vision leads us to take peaceful action and we begin to see evidence of peace in the world we generate around us.

This section contains twelve Value Statements exploring the depth and beauty of those values that the Brahma Kumaris consider essential for the creation of a more just, eco-friendly and peaceful world. These core values have universal application and can improve the quality of life of any individual, organisation, or society that practises them. By changing our awareness, attitude and vision, they have the ability to transform life as we know it.

By defining, describing and distilling the essence of each of the values, we hope that you will be inspired to think about, reflect on, understand, realise, assimilate and practise each one – not only for your own benefit but for the benefit of your family, friends, colleagues and the wider world, including nature.

Since all values are interconnected, to recognise and explore the significance of any one value is to experience the unlimited treasure store of the underlying and supporting values.

CO-OPERATION

It is a fact that in the right formation, the lifting power of many wings can achieve twice the distance of any bird flying alone.
Unknown Source

Those who co-operate receive co-operation. The method to give co-operation is to use the energy of our mind to create vibrations of good wishes and pure feelings for the task and those involved in it. By remaining loving and detached and influenced by our innermost values, rather than external circumstances, strength and wisdom emerge.

Human achievement is like climbing a mountain range with cliffs, crags, slopes and valleys. To reach the peak requires each climber to be equipped with the necessary skills and knowledge as well as inner strength and willpower. However, no climb should ever be undertaken without the most essential piece of equipment – the safety rope of co-operation. Co-operation ensures equanimity, empowerment, easiness and enthusiasm. It enables each climber to take a step, no matter how small, and contribute to the final successful collective outcome.

Mutual Benefit

Co-operation is about working together to achieve a collective goal or aim. It is about going beyond our own limited desires and needs for the greater good. It is not a bargaining game in which our success is achieved at the expense, or exclusion, of the success of others. The constant aim of co-operation is mutual benefit in all our interactions. It is an inclusive process based on the principle of mutual respect. Courage, consideration, caring and sharing provide the foundation from which it develops.

If the power of discrimination is sharp at the time a person, group, or nation needs co-operation and the 'accurate method' is applied, there will be success in our interactions and relationships. The method can be as simple as providing an explanation, giving love or support, or listening. However, if we do not give the right kind of co-operation, in the right way and at the right time, success in the form of agreement and contentment may not be achieved – like the doctor who does not accurately diagnose an illness and, instead of getting well, the patient experiences complications created by the treatment.

Co-operation flourishes when there is a spirit of generosity and sincerity.

This makes us worthy of receiving co-operation from everyone. We have faith and confidence in others and they, in turn, have faith and confidence in us. Together we are able to create an environment of support, empowerment, respect and unity.

Everyone's Responsibility

Co-operation is everyone's responsibility. However, it often requires courage and inner strength to make it happen. Sometimes when we take on this responsibility, we become a target for insult and criticism. In these circumstances, we need to create an internal support mechanism to protect ourselves. By remaining loving and detached and influenced by our innermost values and not external circumstances, subtle co-operation in the form of wisdom emerges. To look at another with an attitude of love and co-operation – even after having been 'defamed' by that person – is known as having merciful vision. Our outlook is infused with understanding, forgiveness, tolerance, patience and empathy and this makes the removal of any challenges, which may have been stalling progress, easier.

Co-operation requires us to recognise the unique role that individuals play and to maintain a sincere and positive attitude towards them. Using the energy of the mind to create vibrations of good wishes and pure feelings for others and the task, affects the atmosphere in a positive and subtle way and prepares the ground for open and profound deliberations and a more successful outcome.

The Time Is Now

By co-operating with time and accepting the natural order of life and events, we develop patience. Time is valuable because it always offers us unique opportunities to achieve what is best and what is necessary, at the moment it is meant to be. Time co-operates with us when we are aware of its importance.

Now is the time for global co-operation. By 'lending a finger of co-operation' each of us can make a real difference to the world – with our mind, our body and our wealth. If each of us were to lend one small finger, together we could lift a mountain!

One day when the subtle ties, which join us together in universal brotherhood, are recognised as unbreakable, co-operation will become inevitable and we will reach new and greater heights!

POINTS FOR REFLECTION

1. *What does 'co-operation' mean to you?*

2. *Think of someone who is an inspiring example of co-operation. What makes them so special? What are the secrets of their success?*

3. *In what ways do you co-operate with other people?*

4. *Are there any areas in your life where you would like to co-operate more with other people? What discourages/prevents you from being more co-operative?*

5. *What could you do to develop your ability to co-operate?*

FREEDOM

No one is free when others are oppressed.
Author Unknown

Full freedom functions only when rights are balanced with responsibilities and choice is balanced with conscience. The most potent power to put an end to internal and external wars is our human conscience.

Freedom is a precious gift. Like an eagle flying in the sky, it promises an experience of liberation and a feeling of no limits – as if the earth, the skies and the seas are ours!

One of the greatest aspirations in the world today is to be free. People want the freedom to lead a life of purpose, to choose a lifestyle in which they and their children can be happy and healthy and flourish through the work of their hands, heads and hearts. They want to do and go as they please and enjoy social, political, economic and religious rights and privileges. In short, they want the freedom to choose, to risk and to succeed on their own terms.

True Freedom

Freedom can be mistakenly understood to be like a blank cheque, which gives us permission to 'do what we like, when we like, to whomever we like'. This idea of freedom is both misleading and an abuse of the right to make choices. If our attention and efforts are focused exclusively on our own rights and choices, at the expense of others, freedom dies.

True freedom is exercised and experienced when parameters, based on the principle that everyone has the same rights, are defined and understood. For example, the right to peace, happiness and justice – regardless of religion, culture, or gender – are innate. To violate the rights of others in order to free the self, family, or nation is a misuse of freedom that usually backfires. It creates conflict and imbalance in the self, others and nature and the result is often much suffering – mentally, physically, spiritually, socially, economically and politically, as can be seen in many places in the world today. To resolve the situation, conditions of constraint and, in some cases, oppression may be imposed on the violated and the violator.

When rights are balanced with responsibilities and choice is balanced with conscience, freedom flourishes, both individually and collectively.

Safeguarding Freedom

To safeguard freedom, we need to be uncompromising. We cannot condone an attitude, which says, for example, "A little greed, a little aggression, a little anger is necessary to keep people in their place." Such thoughts, beginning as a trace of violation, quickly multiply and other wrong sentiments and actions are then justified. Harmful, or negative, thoughts, words, or actions produce equal reactions, as do beneficial and positive thoughts and actions. In other words, we 'reap what we sow'. This natural law of action is known as the 'Law of Karma'. It means that, individually or collectively, positively or negatively, accounts will be created and debts incurred, which will have to be settled one way or another.

One of the key functions of a government, an institution, or any system which has the responsibility to serve, is to safeguard, promote and guarantee freedom at three levels:

1. Individual freedom, including preventing torture, pain or suffering and encouraging self-actualisation and self-expression;

2. Collective freedom, which is demonstrated through justice and equality in human rights for all; and

3. Environmental freedom, which means total respect for the laws of nature, including the rights of all living creatures and the protection of forests, rivers and the earth's atmosphere and resources.

Freedom From Bondage

As trustees of the precious gift of freedom and in response to violations of freedom, we naturally want to liberate peoples and states from the 'iron chains of oppression.' However, even with independence, individuals may remain bound by the 'iron chains' of strong physical desires, anger, greed, attachment and ego and battle internally.

From this 'battlefield' within the self all wars are born.

By honestly acknowledging, accepting and letting go of any negativity within the self, we can free ourselves from the complications and confusion which this battle causes within our mind, intellect and heart. By proactively adopting detachment, lightness and mercy in our consciousness, attitude, words and actions we can break free from our self-created prison of sorrow.

Ultimate freedom is liberation from the bondages created from acting in the consciousness of being just a physical body. Such consciousness causes us to be become attached to the body and its senses, others and worldly possessions. It is the foundation of our fears and insecurities. Going beyond such limitations enables us to be more naturally independent, self-reliant and loving.

Such self-transformation begins the process of world transformation.

The world will only be free from war and injustice when we free ourselves from all the bondages which prevent us from being our true peaceful self.

The most potent power to put an end to all internal and external wars – and to set souls free – is our conscience. Any act of freedom, when aligned with our conscience is liberating, empowering and ennobling.

POINTS FOR REFLECTION

1. *What does 'freedom' mean to you?*

2. *Think of someone who is an inspiring example of the value of freedom. What makes them so special? What are the secrets of their success?*

3. *How good are you at balancing your rights with your responsibilities towards others and the world?*

4. *Are there any areas in your life where you would like to experience greater freedom? What discourages/prevents you from being freer?*

5. *What could you do to develop true freedom in your life?*

HAPPINESS

Happiness resides not in possessions and not in gold. The feeling of happiness dwells in the soul.
Democritus

Through the power of truth there is inner wealth and through the power of peace there is health. Together they give happiness. Happiness is earned by those whose actions, attitude and qualities are pure and selfless.

Paradise, Heaven, Aquarius, El Dorado, the Garden of Eden, the Garden of Allah, Utopia, Vaikunth, the Fields of Osiris and the Golden Age are the names by which a long-gone world of peace, happiness and prosperity has been remembered in different cultures.

In that 'heaven on earth', each human being was like a flower, a country like a bouquet of flowers and the world like a garden of flowers. The sun, the sustainer, shone upon the garden with golden rays, flooding it with newness and nobility. The Gates of Happiness stood open, welcoming the human family to the Golden Garden.

This world was once such a garden and it will become that again.

The Pursuit of Happiness

At present, many people question the purpose of their life. Some are tired of living; others have lost hope. Some make effort to earn wealth, believing that it will bring them happiness. Others who are wealthy may not be healthy and that causes distress. Some choose a certain profession, believing that it will give them happiness, while others seek happiness through relationships. Such external, material sources of happiness are temporary and limited and, ultimately, not completely satisfying. In many instances, they are a source of unhappiness and sorrow.

The inability to hold on to pure and lasting happiness results from a bankruptcy of spiritual values and powers.

It is the awareness and application of spiritual truths that provides the true source of happiness.

Through the power of truth there is wealth. Through the power of peace there is health. Together they give happiness. Like a tonic, spiritual knowledge makes hopeless ones hopeful. Pure happiness returns to anyone who seeks such new and hopeful horizons. Important things that have been forgotten are remembered. The feeling can be compared to returning home – as you see the trees and smell the breeze, you know you are nearing something close to your heart!

The warmth and comfort of happiness is hidden within the self. *When we turn within and take strength from the internal powers of peace and silence, we revive our virtues and allow our mercury of happiness to rise.* The soul becomes open to the secrets of how to live in an interdependent way without becoming a victim of the material world, which by its very nature robs people of their happiness.

The vault of spiritual knowledge holds many treasures that enable us to live and act with truth. These include guidelines on how to reform our character and activities, the most important which is purity. Purity is the mother of happiness and comfort. Clear, clean and positive thoughts, feelings, words and actions are the keys which unlock the Gates of Happiness; they are the foundation of self-progress and personal transformation bringing strength and contentment to the self and pleasure to others.

Happiness of Mind

Happiness of mind is a state of peace in which there is no upheaval or violence. Such peace within the self creates faith in the intellect. The flute of happiness plays softly and constantly in the minds of those who have such faith. No matter how adverse, or challenging, a situation may be, there is fearlessness because the power of faith gives the guarantee of ultimate victory. As the intellect becomes enlightened by spiritual wisdom, there are less mood swings and doubts in the heart. We become more able to pay off debts of pain and sorrow and realise that the greatest secret about being happy is: *Give happiness and take happiness. Do not give sorrow or take sorrow.*

Happiness is a form of nourishment which comes from 'self-sovereignty', that is being the master of our mind, intellect, personality traits and the physical senses of the body. In other words, being 'complete', full of all powers and virtues with a perfect balance between masculine and feminine characteristics. This state of perfection lies deep within each soul.

In the search for this perfection, our intellect goes through a process of discovering its divine nature.

Unlimited Fortune

Happiness is priceless. It cannot be bought, sold, or bargained for. It is earned when our actions, attitude and attributes are pure and selfless.

Social, economic and political stability are often cited as sources of happiness and enjoyment in life. Yet, whenever any one of these areas is in disarray, people's happiness drops. When resources are focused on the socioeconomic infrastructure at the expense of the development of the spiritual and moral character of the people, priorities in life are distorted and there is a gradual erosion of happiness.

Using moral and spiritual values, we can, if we wish, reassess our priorities and take positive, proactive and preventive measures to restore the balance.

The road to happiness is paved with golden opportunities. Each footstep taken on the journey is guaranteed to bring great benefit to the self and others. When we walk the path together there is even greater happiness. Through our collective actions we can once more open the Golden Gate of the world.

POINTS FOR REFLECTION

1. *What does 'happiness' mean to you?*

2. *Think of someone who is an inspiring example of happiness. Write a list of the ways in which they demonstrate their happiness? What are the secrets of their success?*

3. *In what ways do you express your happiness?*

4. *Are there any areas in your life where you would like to be happier? What discourages/prevents you from being happier?*

5. *What could you do to develop greater happiness in your life?*

HONESTY

The saying that 'honesty is the best policy' has met with the just criticism that honesty is not a policy. The real honest man is honest from conviction of what is right, not from policy.
Robert E. Lee

Honesty means there are no contradictions or discrepancies in our thoughts, words, or actions. To be honest to our real self and to the purpose of a task earns trust and inspires faith in others. Honesty is never to misuse that which is given in trust.

Honesty is having a clear conscience 'before myself and before my fellow human beings'. It is about doing what is right and appropriate in our roles, behaviour and relationships. We say what we think and do what we say. There are no contradictions, or discrepancies, in our thoughts, words, or actions; no hypocrisy or artificiality to create confusion and mistrust in the minds and lives of others; no barriers to prevent us being close to others. Honesty makes for a life of integrity because the inner and outer selves are a mirror image.

Honesty is as distinct as a flawless diamond. It can never remain hidden. Its worth is visible in our actions. Being the same on the outside as on the inside, we are authentic and have integrity, one of the most valued of human qualities. Such integration provides clarity and we become an example to others.

Clouding Issues

Inner honesty needs to be examined in order to provide wisdom and support and ensure strength and stability. We need courage and determination, as well as spiritual knowledge and awareness, to understand who we really are.

We also need to:

○ recognise and accept our strengths and weaknesses

○ realise the importance of being true to our own unique blend of values, qualities, talents and specialities

○ be aligned to the purpose of our life.

Accepting, appreciating, valuing and nurturing our innate inner goodness increases our self-esteem and gives us stability, strength and confidence. We become less dependent on others for approval and we are able to assert ourselves when necessary.

Dishonesty may arise if internally there is any attachment to a person, object, or idea. Such attachment becomes an obstacle to reality and objectivity and it is harder to take action in the interests of the whole. Any negative feelings, habits, selfish motives or hidden agendas are like stains on the mirror of our life. Honesty acts as a stain remover.

For self-growth, there needs to be cleanliness in our efforts and truth in our heart.

Cleanliness means exploring and changing those aspects of our consciousness and activity which blemish the self and raise doubts in others. Without honesty in the head and heart there will be self-deception or a tendency for us to deceive others by clouding issues with excuses or long-winded explanations! When the mirror of the self is clean, our feelings, nature, motives and objectives are transparent and we become trustworthy.

To be trusted and to trust provides the foundation and cohesion necessary for all good relationships.

When we are able to openly share our feelings and motives with others there is closeness. Without honesty and trust there is mistrust and tension and neither individuals nor societies can function effectively. Honesty and trust are the foundation of happy marriages, healthy democracies, successful businesses and economies, flourishing religions and peace between nations and people.

At this time the world is crying out for honesty.

Application and Experimentation

The personal and collective application of these ethics and principles involves experimenting to see what works best i.e. what is meaningful and useful. Progress comes through experimenting with honesty and implementing it as completely and sincerely as possible at any given moment. When there is the experience of success, commitment to honesty and integrity is strengthened.

To carry out a task out of force or compulsion, or with a careless or selfish attitude does not reflect pure motives and will cause a negative reaction. To be honest with our real self and true to the purpose of a task earns trust and inspires faith in others. Purity of motive and consistency of effort sustain our progress.

An honest person is someone who aspires to follow the highest codes of conduct, who is loyal to the benevolent and universal principles of life and whose decisions are based clearly on what is right and wrong.

In practice, this means being fair, keeping our word and standing up for what we believe in. It also means putting an end to stealing and cheating, or playing off one person against another for our own advantage and 'ripping people off'.

Honesty means to 'be good and do good', even at the expense of our own comfort and well-being if necessary. To do otherwise is demoralising and depressing, individually and collectively – a recipe for chaos and conflict.

Honesty also means never misusing, abusing, or wasting that which is given in trust. For example, the world's natural resources which are provided for the well-being of *all* humanity. When these resources are used in a worthwhile way to satisfy the basic human, moral and spiritual needs of all people, there is a sense of well-being, harmony and unity, which is the foundation of social, political and economic stability

People who are deeply committed to development and progress keep honesty as a constant principle in their efforts to build a world of peace and plenty, free from corruption.

POINTS FOR REFLECTION

1. *What does 'honesty' mean to you?*

2. *Think of someone who is an inspiring example of integrity. What makes them so special? What are the secrets of their success?*

3. *In what ways are you honest with yourself and others?*

4. *Are there any areas in your life where you would like to be more honest? What prevents you from achieving this?*

5. *What could you do to develop greater honesty in your life?*

※

HUMILITY

Life is a long lesson in humility.
James Matthew Barrie

To embody humility means to make the effort to listen to and accept others. The more we do this, the more we will be held in high esteem and the more we will be listened to. One word spoken in humility has the impact of a thousand words.

Humility is found in the still inner ocean of the self. Just as exploration can lead to buried treasures, when we search our inner world we can find jewels buried in the depths. And the jewel buried deepest – which shines the brightest and gives the most light – is humility. At the darkest moments, its rays penetrate. It removes fear and insecurity and opens us up to universal truths.

Trusteeship

Humility is based on an understanding that everything we have – from the bodies we were born into, to our most prized possessions – is inherited and that as human beings we are all subject to the same natural and spiritual laws.

Each of us is a trustee on a journey of self-discovery with the ability to make our own decisions and learn from the consequences of our actions. We cannot claim credit for the gifts we have been given for the journey – our gender, race, appearance, intellectual ability, values and qualities. However, it is good to acknowledge and appreciate our gifts, be grateful for them and use them in a worthwhile and benevolent way for the self and others.

The consciousness of being a trustee of such unlimited and timeless resources touches the core of the human soul and awakens it to the realisation that, just as at the time of birth such resources were inherited, at the time of death they will be left behind. When we die all that will accompany us will be the impressions of how we used our gifts and the wisdom learned from having been and lived as a trustee.

The consciousness of being a trustee heightens our self-esteem and improves our relationships. It encourages silent reflection, inviting us to take time out to look at life from a different perspective and consider better ways of relating to the self (including how we use our mind and body), others and the world.

Removing 'I' and 'Mine'

The consciousness of 'I' and 'mine' lies at the heart of most conflict. Possessiveness over an idea or belief, a role, an activity, an object, a person, even the physical body leads to attachment. We then hold on to what we have and go to great lengths to protect it, often against all reason and the universal values which give worth and meaning to life.

Humility allows us to 'let go and let be'. It enables us to go beyond arrogance and ego and eliminate the possessiveness and narrow vision, which create physical, intellectual and emotional boundaries, destroy our self-esteem and distance us from others. By putting others first, humility gently works on the crevices to allow for breakthroughs in our relationships.

Humility enables us to become dependable, flexible and adaptable. We make the effort to listen to and accept others. The more we do this, the more we will be listened to and the more we will be held in high esteem.

The extent to which we become humble is the degree to which we become great in everyone's heart.

A Call to Serve

Humility is an essential quality in serving others. *The greater our humility, the greater will be our success.* We cannot bring benefit to the world or build civil societies without humility. Serving others is most effective when:

1. We regard ourselves as a trustee, or an instrument; and

2. We take the first step towards accepting others who are different.

When we are humble we are able to function in all environments, no matter how unfamiliar or negative. Our attitude, outlook, words, connections and relationships create an inviting, cordial, comfortable, non-threatening atmosphere. Our words are essenceful, powerful and spoken with good manners and we can defuse another's anger with just a few words. One word spoken in humility has the impact of a thousand words.

On the high tides of human interactions, humility is like a lighthouse. If our mind and intellect are clear, humility enables us to act as a detached observer. We are able to see the bigger picture, perceive situations, discern the causes of obstacles and difficulties and yet remain silent. When we do express an opinion, it is with an open mind and recognition of the specialities, strengths and sensitivities of our self and others.

Humility is also an essential ingredient in our relationship with nature. As trustees we respect the laws of nature realising that to arrogantly exploit and damage the natural habitat is to put the whole world, including the entire human family, in peril.

POINTS FOR REFLECTION

1. *What does 'humility' mean to you?*

2. *Think of someone who is an inspiring example of humility. What makes them so special? What are the secrets of their success?*

3. *In what ways do you demonstrate the value of humility in your life?*

4. *Are there any areas in your life where you would like to be more humble? What discourages/prevents you from being more humble?*

5. *How could you achieve greater humility in your life?*

LOVE

We look forward to the time when the power of love will replace the love of power. Then will our world know the blessings of peace.

William E. Gladstone

Love is the principle which creates and sustains all our relationships, giving them dignity and depth. Spiritual love takes us into silence and that silence has the power to unite, guide and free people. Love is the bedrock for the belief in equality of spirit and personhood. Love combined with faith creates a strong foundation for initiative and action.

Love is not simply a desire, a passion, an intense feeling for one person or object, but a consciousness, which is simultaneously selfless and self-fulfilling.

Love is having good wishes and pure feelings for everyone and everything. Love flows from truth, that is, spiritual wisdom. Love based on wisdom is real love, not blind love.

To discover the secrets of love is to watch the secrets of life unfold.

The Eternal Flame

Human beings have become caught up in a pattern of behaviour which has distorted the value of love and our ability to trust one another with our feelings and intentions. One minute there is love; the next minute that love is broken, resulting in intense sorrow and pain. It is as if our intellect has lost connection with the One eternal source of love and has taken support from temporary sources. As a result, instead of having one strength and one support from an unconditional Source, we remain thirsty for true love and wander around in distress, searching for it

The world remembers God as the ultimate Source of love, the Ocean of Love, the Eternal Flame. God gives – unconditionally – love that is imperishable, unlimited and unique:

❍ *Imperishable* – eternal, constantly radiating and totally available;

❍ *Unlimited* – without boundaries or preferences; loving vibrations emanate to all souls regardless of culture, race or creed;

❍ *Unique* – in that the fire of God's love cleans the heart and soul.

When we tap into this love through meditation we re-establish the bond of an eternal relationship. When we experience God's love and 'merge with the Eternal Flame of Truth', we disconnect from falsehood and learn the first lesson of universal brotherhood – that we are all children of the same Parent and, as such, we are all brothers and sisters, part of one family. This understanding is the foundation of spiritual love.

The Basis of True Love

The basis of real love between people is spirituality. To see another as a spiritual being, a soul, is to see the reality of the other. Maintaining this awareness creates a spiritual relationship in which each person, complete within, independent yet totally interconnected, recognises that state in the other. As a result, there is constant and natural love.

Such love is eternal, as the soul never dies. Such love brings joy whilst attachment to that which is perishable brings sorrow.

Love is the catalyst for change, development and achievement.

In the presence of true love, neither internal nor external animosity, hatred, anger or jealousy are possible. Negative feelings are transformed into positive ones and controlling, or co-dependent, tendencies are replaced by kindness, care and understanding. Harmony prevails.

The Coolness of Love

Spiritual love means not dwelling on the weaknesses of others. Instead, there is concern for removing our own defects. The method to do this is to 'check our own pulse' regularly and monitor how much we have adopted the natural habit of giving happiness, rather than sorrow, to others.

True effort means to remove whatever weaknesses stand in the way of love.

In our relationships with others, we 'see but do not see' and 'hear but do not hear' anything negative. We maintain the highest vision and regard for them. If necessary we correct what is inaccurate with a feeling of love and the power of words. There needs to be a balance between the two. When there is too much force in the words or too much love, the result is not successful. If the words are too sharp, the other may be insulted or put off by bossiness. When we have the right balance the other experiences compassion, mercy and benefit – no matter how powerful or challenging the message, it will touch their heart and inspire them to change.

When the fire of spiritual love has been ignited, we begin exercising the willpower to set ourselves free from the bondages of short-lived gratification. Time is invested and effort is made to build an internal stage in which love is revealed on our face and in all our activities. Knowing we are not alone, we are less disturbed by adverse circumstances. We view dark clouds and storms as opportunities to exercise our internal strength and resources and grow in love. Seeing the benefit in everything we do not step away from a particular person, place, or task. Instead, we have the faith that, with effort, we will make a significant and beneficial difference. The more effort we make to love, the more love is received.

The entire world can be transformed through our loving vision, attitude and actions.

To create a better world – a world of truth – spiritual love is essential. In a better world, the natural law is love; and in a better person, their natural nature is loving.

POINTS FOR REFLECTION

1. *What does 'love' mean to you?*

2. *Think of someone who is an inspiring example of love. What makes them so special? What are the secrets of their success?*

3. *In what ways do you demonstrate love in your life?*

4. *Are there any areas in your life where you would like to be more loving? What discourages/prevents you from being more loving?*

5. *How could you achieve greater love in your life?*

PEACE

Let us forgive each other – only then will we live in peace.
Leo Tolstoy

In its purest form, peace is inner silence filled with the power of truth. Peace is the prominent characteristic of what we call 'a civilized society' and the character of a society can be seen through the collective consciousness of its members.

The challenge to peace normally presents itself in the question, "Are human beings by nature violent or non-violent?" If the answer is violent, then the concept of peace becomes nonexistent. Peace has become so elusive that people have begun to question its existence. 'Peace of mind' has become a popular cliché, but what does it mean?

What Is Peace?

Peace is a positive, powerful qualitative energy, which emanates constantly from the one imperishable Source. Peace consists of pure thoughts, pure feelings and pure wishes. It penetrates the shell of chaos and by its very nature automatically puts things and people into balanced order. It is the balm of human relationships and a source of comfort and strength in times of trouble.

Peace is the absence of fear and tension, dislike and distaste and the presence of good-will and loving-kindness. It is a form of gentle awareness that seeks to understand and heal rather than judge and condemn.

The Original Quality of the Soul

The self is a reservoir of vital resources, one of which is peace. To recognize the original quality of the human soul as peace is to stop searching outside for peace. Through connection with the one eternal and unlimited Source of peace, our own reservoirs overflow

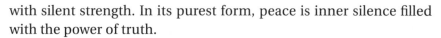

with silent strength. In its purest form, peace is inner silence filled with the power of truth.

To exercise the power of peace we need to understand and embrace the fundamental principle of spirituality, that is to look inward in order to look outward with courage, purpose and meaning.

The first step in that process requires taking responsibility for, and carefully examining, our thoughts, feelings and motives. By opening the door to the inner self, through silent reflection, contemplation and meditation, we are able to clarify and pinpoint those attitudes and behaviour patterns, which are destructive and cause chaos and sorrow and change them.

When the energy of our thoughts, words and actions is balanced and stable, we experience peace in the self, in our relationships and with the world. We are able to stay cool, calm and collected in any situation and *respond* rather than *react* to the internal and external influences that could disturb our peace of mind.

The foundation of peace is non-violence to the self, others and nature.

Peace is a constant practice which uses the support of other virtues, such as patience, compassion, acceptance and forgiveness. It requires us to be the master of our sense organs in order to conquer the spiritual diseases of lust (in all its many forms), anger, greed, attachment and ego, which lie at the heart of all peacelessness.

To become a messenger of peace is no small thing. It requires considerable inner power, self-discipline, determination and the courage to stand out in the crowd.

The Search For Peace

People say in one breath that they want peace of mind and in the next breath they say hurtful things. Wasteful gossip spreads peacelessness, as does anger. Peacelessness initially begins with a few angry, forceful thoughts, which are then expressed in words, which then, in some instances, escalate into uncontrolled violence.

People say they want peace in the world, but what kind of peace do they desire? They ask for peace, but whose responsibilityit to create peace? Can anyone who remains peaceless be an instrument for peace? Fighting for peace is a contradiction in terms.

Authenticity of action depends on the authenticity of the person.

In its most common form, peacelessness can be experienced as stress and pressure due to family, work, social and other obligations. In its more serious condition, peacelessness is manifested in breakdowns, addictions, abuse, crime, emotional imbalances and psychosomatic ailments. While medical science has helped relieve symptoms of stress and psychology has contributed towards understanding the psyche, there is a growing genuine search for a functional and empowering spirituality, which can produce within the individual a calm and relaxed state of mind.

The inner qualities and thought power of human beings are fast being recognized as tools to deal with the world and its growing demands. Health is being examined from a holistic perspective, partnering both physical and spiritual energies in the process of healing. Even when physical health is maintained, spiritual resources are being tapped to enhance coping skills and interpersonal relations.

Overcoming Anger

One of the main enemies of peace is anger. Like a virus, it lives within the hearts and minds of us all and takes many forms from mild irritation to boiling rage. Pulled by resentment and harboured hurts we find ourselves reacting, either passively or aggressively, to the 'triggers' of people, situations or circumstances that activate the pain of the past.

Fighting fire with fire does not work. There is a better way. Just as the forces of anger have accumulated drop by drop, so too can the forces of peace. By having the honesty and courage to face, acknowledge, accept and let go of the pain within and the other things that disturb and annoy us, we can heal ourselves. In this process we need to exercise wisdom, patience, love, compassion, understanding, forgiveness and mercy.

Choosing the path of peace, instead of the path of anger, pain and sorrow, provides us with an opportunity to learn and grow and make a real contribution to world peace. Like throwing a pebble in the pond, the power of our example ripples out and inspires others to do likewise. By 'walking the talk' we can make a real difference. Just like the Buddha.

The Promise of Peace

Peace is the foundation, the major building block upon which a healthy functioning society stands. Peace is the prominent characteristic of what we call 'a civilised society'. The character of a society can be seen through the collective consciousness of its members. A civilisation can be heaven, or hell, depending on the consciousness of its members. Consciousness creates culture – its norms, values and systems – and consciousness can transform culture.

At the present time, the world is crying out for 'Peace on Earth'. We seem to be living in a sea of conflict, injustice, misunderstanding, ignorance and prejudice where fighting, criticism, complaining and blaming others is the order of the day. Many people feel hopeless and helpless victims of oppressive systems, which seem beyond their control and they feel a need to hit out at others.

Politicians and policy-makers everywhere are dedicated to making, building and keeping peace. A tremendous amount of human resources and research is being invested in establishing peace in the world. Even peace prizes are given to people for their work towards peace. Emphasis is placed on the value of peace precisely because of the great peacelessness that exists everywhere – it has infiltrated our lives far deeper than we care to admit.

Peace Gives Hope

The promise of peace gives hope but like a piece of quicksilver, it sometimes seems slippery and evasive. We are at a crossroads of human civilisation. On the one hand, things are rapidly disintegrating. That is made bitterly apparent by the wars, civil strife, riots, ethnic cleansing and acts of terrorism which are tearing the world apart. However, on the other hand, an almost invisible integration, involving alternatives and possibilities, is putting the pieces together.

Bringing peace back into the social, economic, political and other fibres of society requires looking at peace from two levels: the *external* and the *internal*.

Peace education, conflict resolution and all peace initiatives must take seriously the critical connection between individual consciousness and world peace. Programmes and projects must include an emphasis on individual peace, offering proactive and practical means to peace, beginning with the first step of knowing, accepting and experiencing the peace that lies within the heart of each one of us, however angry, hateful or murderous we may appear to be.

Ultimately, peace will come when all minds and hearts are simultaneously focused and stabilised on the one imperishable Source of peace. Then the reverberation of peace emitting from the silence will echo, 'World Peace Is Declared!'

POINTS FOR REFLECTION

1. *What does 'peace' mean to you?*

2. *Think of someone who is an inspiring example of peace. What makes them so special? What are the secrets of their success?*

3. *In what ways do you demonstrate peace in your life?*

4. *Are there any areas in your life where you would like to be more peaceful? What discourages/prevents you from being more peaceful?*

5. *How could you become more peaceful?*

RESPECT

When you are content to be simply yourself and do not compare or compete, everybody will respect you.
Lao Tzu

To know one's own worth and to honour the worth of others is the true way to earn respect. Respect is an acknowledgment of the inherent worth and innate rights of the individual and the collective. These must be recognised as the central focus to draw from people a commitment to a higher purpose in life.

Respect is having the highest regard for someone or something – really valuing and appreciating their intrinsic worth. All respect begins within the self, recognising the power and unlimited potential that lies within what has been described as the last frontier, i.e. the miracle and mystery of the being within the body. This being is variously referred to as a 'point of light', a 'divine spark', 'higher consciousness', the 'life force', the 'spirit' or the 'soul'.

Our original state of self-respect is based on the awareness of this inner self as a unique, precious entity, which, when it first enters a body, is complete and perfect and full of all powers. It is pure energy and radiates absolute peace, love and joy. Lacking nothing, it gives all – like a shining star or a tiny sparkling diamond.

At this moment in time, we may feel far removed from this elevated state of being, which lies deeply buried within our sub-conscious mind. However, through meditation, contemplation, reflection or prayer, it is possible to remember and reconnect with this inner truth and re-emerge it in our life.

When we experience this elevated consciousness (often referred to as 'self-realisation') we develop faith in the self and a feeling of wholeness and completeness within. This is true self-respect. Based on who we are, rather than what we do, it colours not only our view of our self but of all human beings who, regardless of their creed, colour or behaviour, share the same spiritual nature and make-up.

Beneath all the external differences, we are all spiritual brothers.

The Challenge

Self-respect is the foundation of self-confidence and self esteem. It gives us the courage to stand up for our rights and to assert ourselves when necessary. It enables us to create happy, healthy relationships based on equality and mutual regard rather than fear or force. Knowing our true worth, there is no need to impress, dominate, compete, or cover up our inadequacies with arrogance, false pride or an obsequious humility. We give our best and do our best because we want to, rather than because we have to.

Being content and satisfied with ourselves, we appreciate the unique worth of others and their right to be themselves. Like different flowers in a garden, we all have a right to bloom. Such a mindset guarantees success since interaction, on this basis, assures that the inherent goodness of the self and the other will emerge, sooner or later.

Conflict arises when the awareness of our original nature and that of others is lacking. This happens when we leave the seat of our self-respect.

When the word 'self' is removed from self-respect, the void is filled by a variety of desires or expectations designed to claim regard or respect from others. When we become dependent on external forces rather than internal powers, we tend to measure respect in terms of physical and material factors, such as appearance, income, status and popularity. 'I' and 'mine' become the order of the day. The more we measure our respect on the basis of these temporary external labels, the greater will be our desire for such recognition from others and the more likely we are to fall and lose the respect of ourselves and others.

To know our own worth and to honour the worth of others is the true way to earn respect. Since such a principle originates in that pristine place of pure worth, others instinctively sense its authenticity and sincerity. In the vision and attitude of equality, there is shared spirituality. Sharing creates a sense of belonging, a feeling of family.

If we stabilise ourselves in our elevated awareness of self-respect, then the regard of others will follow like a shadow.

To develop such respect within the self and to express it in our daily life is one of our greatest challenges. Obstacles come to test the strength of our respect and self-reliance, often at the most vulnerable of times.

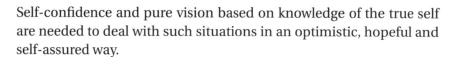

Self-confidence and pure vision based on knowledge of the true self are needed to deal with such situations in an optimistic, hopeful and self-assured way.

Respect and Humility

Humility is the companion of true self-respect. Although we appreciate and enjoy our original nature, we cannot claim credit for it, any more than we claim credit for being tall or good-looking. It is just the way we are. When respect for the self is balanced with this humility we are able to value individuality and appreciate diversity, whether political, religious or cultural. This balance of humility and self-respect results in selfless service. We perform honourable actions devoid of debilitating attitudes such as arrogance and narrow-mindedness, which damage, or destroy, the uniqueness of others and violate their fundamental rights. Such attitudes hurt us as well as the other.

Respect is an acknowledgment of the inherent worth and innate rights of the self and the collective. These must be recognised as the central focus to draw from people a commitment to a higher purpose in life.

The eminence of life is present in everyone and every human being has a right to the joy of living with respect and dignity.

Respect for Nature

The splendour and mystery of the human soul is matched only by the power and glory of Nature. The abundance and beauty of nature and the wonder of its finely tuned, inter-related mechanisms on which we depend for our survival and well-being, fully deserve our greatest respect, appreciation and gratitude. However, the forces of urbanisation, industrialisation and relentless consumerism have broken the bond between us and much of our behaviour shows a complete lack of respect for the Earth, its seas and animal and plant kingdoms. Almost everything is up for grabs to be used and abused by the highest bidder regardless of the consequences. To show such disrespect and to work against the laws of nature is causing huge ecological imbalances and many natural calamities. Only when we once more give respect and reverence to the eternal energy of matter, will the relationship be healed and the elements serve humanity with accuracy and abundance.

POINTS FOR REFLECTION

1. *What does 'respect' mean to you?*

2. *Think of someone who is an inspiring example of respect. What makes them so special? What are the secrets of their success?*

3. *In what ways do you demonstrate respect for yourself, others and nature?*

4. *Are there any areas in your life where you would like to be more respectful? What discourages or prevents you from doing this?*

5. *How could you develop the value of respect in your life?*

RESPONSIBILITY

When you blame others, you give up your power to change.
Anon

A responsible person fulfils the assigned duty by staying true to the aim. Duties are carried out with integrity and a sense of purpose.

Circumstances, necessity and choice place us in particular situations and roles. Our moral *response-ability* is to honour the role which has been entrusted to us. We should not wish to be someone else or be somewhere else but accept what is required and perform it conscientiously and to the best of our ability, with integrity and a sense of purpose.

Our First Responsibility

Our first duty and responsibility is to the self; to take responsibility for our own life – for the body we have been given, as well as the thoughts, words and actions we perform through the body.

If we do not look after ourselves who will? If we do not keep ourselves fit and healthy on all levels (spiritual, mental, emotional and physical), how are we going to fulfil our other responsibilities and make a positive contribution to the world of family, friends, work and beyond?

If we wish to be an instrument for positive change in this deteriorating world, we need to lead by example and develop a loving relationship with the self and others based on honesty, respect and many of the other values mentioned in this book. By building up our inner strength and protecting ourselves from external negative influences, especially the attractions and distractions of modern consumerism and technology, we will become the change we want to see.

Acting Responsibly

Personal responsibility in life comes from many expected and unexpected sources and involves partnership and participation, commitment and co-operation. Social and global responsibility also requires justice, humanity and respect for the rights of *all* human beings without discrimination.

Section 1

Some people interpret responsibility as a burden and fail to see it as personally relevant, projecting it as someone else's problem.

A responsible person perseveres, not stubbornly with a blind focus, but with the motivation of fulfilling the assigned duty by staying true to the aim. When there is the consciousness of being an instrument, or a facilitator, we stay neutral and flexible in our role, detached yet with a clear understanding of what needs to be done. When we play the role accurately, there is efficiency and effectiveness and, as a result, we feel satisfied and content at having made a significant contribution.

Responsibility often requires humility to help overcome obstacles created by the ego. For example, acting responsibly does not mean taking over, or controlling, the outcome. Acting responsibly does mean having the maturity to know when a responsibility should be handed to another. A major barrier to success is becoming too attached to the responsibility. Being over-conscientious leads to worry, doubt and fear, which can have a crippling effect on our decision-making ability and result in harmful consequences.

Collaboration is Essential

Responsible individuals work in collaboration with others. That is true for all tasks but especially in areas which affect the lives of others. Responsible individuals operate on the premises that:

○ Everyone has something worthwhile to offer;

○ The situation requires a co-operative rather than a competitive approach.

Responsible people do not fall into the traps of inferiority or superiority; they recognise that the optimum outcome cannot depend on just one person, one group, or one nation alone.

Responsibility is managing our time and resources to bring maximum benefit whilst accommodating necessary change.

Decisions made in the consciousness of being responsible for social or global welfare encourage actions which are performed in a selfless way. In taking responsibility for others' rights, a budget of all assets – mental, physical and spiritual – needs to be devised, including the available resources and their efficient and equitable use.

Inattention, carelessness, corruption, greed, or a lack of judgment may result in some people, or areas, receiving nothing, some not enough and others too much as well as the unnecessary loss of human lives and natural resources.

Accountability

When people perform actions for individual or world improvement, they need an internal support system, such as meditation or reflection, to help them assimilate and put into practice the necessary qualities required for success. This is particularly true for role models such as parents, educators, religious and political leaders, celebrities and opinion leaders, who help shape the norms, which have an enormous influence on the fabric of society.

One principle of learning is observing the behaviour and real-life experience of those we admire and respect. Therefore, it is incumbent upon role models to accept and honour the responsibility of being 'examples'. The bigger the part, the greater the concern should be for the message being imparted and its impact on the lives of others.

With rights go responsibilities and within that concept the law of action and reaction is operable. Life is the field of action and on that field our part should be enacted with responsibility and accountability.

Each human being is like a star consisting of his or her own small world. We have to check our world and look for the balance of rights and responsibilities. When we wear the crown of responsibility embedded with the jewels of rights, we become stars of success with a positive influence on the world.

POINTS FOR REFLECTION

1. *What does 'responsibility' mean to you?*

2. *Think of someone who is an inspiring example of responsibility. What makes them so special? What are the secrets of their success?*

3. *In what ways do you demonstrate the value of responsibility in your life?*

4. *Are there any areas in your life where you would like to be more responsible? What discourages/prevents you from doing this?*

5. *How could you develop the value of responsibility in your life?*

SIMPLICITY

Purity and simplicity are the two wings with which man soars above the earth and all temporary nature.

Thomas Kempis

Simplicity brings clarity and peace of mind to our constantly changing and highly complex world. Simplicity is the conscience, which calls upon us to rethink our values.

Simplicity grows from sacred roots, embodying a wealth of spiritual virtues and values, which are made apparent in our attitude, words, activities and lifestyle. Simplicity is natural. It may appear common and without appeal to those whose vision has become superficial but to those with an artist's refined insight, it is the essence of beauty and truth.

Simple Living, High Thinking

Simplicity is having a clean and clear mind and intellect. Simplicity combines sweetness and wisdom. When we live with simplicity, we are free from unnecessary and complicated thinking; our intellect is sharp and alert and we have the insight and intuition to create concise thoughts and empathetic feelings. There is no ego in simplicity. We are able to renounce possessiveness and be free from material desires, which distract the intellect, causing it to wander into wasteful territory. Being without desire does not mean we go without. On the contrary, we have everything, including inner fulfilment. This is apparent on our face – innocent of disturbance, weakness and anger – and in our behaviour – uniquely elegant and royal, yet child-like. Simplicity is being both the innocent child and the wise master. It teaches us plain living and high thinking.

People who live simply usually enjoy a close relationship with nature. Their ethic is derived from perennial traditions operating according to the laws of nature. They rise at dawn and retire at dusk. They tell the time of day by the position of the sun and determine the dates of sacred days by the position of the moon. Herbs become their natural cures, the backyard their farmer's market and the moon and stars their light bulbs. The natural world is their classroom. This does not mean that we should all adopt such a lifestyle! However, there are lessons to be learned in nature.

When the ethic of simplicity is followed, there is hardly any waste.

All resources, time, thoughts, ideas, knowledge, money and raw materials are valued as investments and used in a worthwhile way. With more economy and less splendour we can create a clutter-free life style in which less is more.

From Simplicity Grows Generosity

By sharing our resources in a congenial and caring manner, we restore the meaning of *family* to human activity. However, simplicity is more than giving money and material possessions. It is about giving that of the self, which is priceless – our patience, friendship and encouragement. When we donate our time freely to others with kindness, openness and pure intentions, without expectations and conditions, we reap the abundant fruits sown from the seeds of our generous actions.

Beauty is Truth

Simplicity is truth. The beauty of truth is so simple; it works like alchemy. No matter how many disguises may come in front of it, the light of truth cannot remain hidden; it will reach out to the masses in a language so simple yet with a message so profound.

The messengers of truth have always embodied ordinary forms, led simple lives and adopted simple ways of imparting their messages. They have lived and spoken their truth, bringing hope, clarity and beauty to the lives of others. In their simplicity and splendour, they can be compared to a jeweller who makes every single jewel flawless and precious, whilst himself remaining simple.

Today beauty is defined by the fashion and beauty industries, amplified by the rich and famous and embraced by the masses. However, beauty, in its simplest form, is about removing the arrogance of expensive clothing and extravagant living. It goes beyond rich and poor. It is about appreciating the small things in life, sometimes not visible or apparent to the rest of the world.

Simplicity is appreciating our own and others' inner beauty and recognising the value of everyone, even the poorest and worst off. It is considering all tasks, including the most menial, to have worth and dignity.

Ethic of Simplicity

The ethic of simplicity is the precursor to sustainable development. Simplicity teaches us economy, to be clear and honest about our needs and live accordingly. Simplicity is the conscience that calls upon us to rethink our values and ask whether we are being induced to purchase unnecessary products.

It has been said that the Earth provides enough resources to satisfy 'our needs but not our greed' (Gandhi). Psychological enticements create artificial needs. Desires stimulated by wanting unnecessary 'things' result in value clashes complicated by greed, fear, peer pressure and a false sense of identity. Extremes and excesses invite overindulgence and waste. Although such an approach can be defended as a means to build and grow certain economies, it should not be done at the expense of pushing other economies into dire poverty.

The imposed sacrifice of some for the greater affluence of others is not a principle but an injustice, which has serious consequences for us all, politically, economically and environmentally.

Simplicity helps decrease the gap between 'the haves' and 'the have nots' by demonstrating the logic of true economics which is to earn, save, invest and share the sacrifices and the prosperity so that there is a better quality of life for *all* people regardless of where they live.

POINTS FOR REFLECTION

1. *What does 'simplicity' mean to you?*

2. *Think of someone who is an inspiring example of simplicity. What makes them so special? What are the secrets of their success?*

3. *In what ways do you demonstrate the value of simplicity in your life?*

4. *Are there any areas in your life where you would like to live a more simple life? What discourages/prevents you from doing this?*

5. *How could you develop the value of simplicity in your life?*

TOLERANCE

Through the centuries, the history of peoples is but a lesson in mutual tolerance.

Emile Zola

Through understanding and open-mindedness, we attract others who are different and by genuinely accepting and accommodating them, we demonstrate tolerance in a practical form.

Tolerance is based on a deep understanding, an inner knowing, that as human beings we are all brothers and sisters, part of one global family; that we are connected in many ways just like the leaves, limbs, branches and trunk of a tree.

On the human world tree, each limb represents a nation, the branches represent the various provinces and communities of religions and ethnic groups and each human being is a leaf on the tree. Since a tree takes sustenance from common, original roots, which grew from one seed, the human family tree can be no different. Coexistence stems from the very seed from which life sprang.

To attack or destroy even one limb of the tree is to spoil the whole tree just as fights and quarrels in a family adversely affect the whole family.

Coexistence

The aim of tolerance is peaceful coexistence. Tolerance recognises and accepts individuality *and* diversity; it removes divisive masks and defuses the tension created by ignorance. It allows us to discover and dissolve the stereotypes and stigmas associated with people perceived to be 'different' because of their race, nationality, religion, gender, sexual orientation, disability, or heritage.

Just as a gardener recognises the characteristics of each variety of seed and prepares the ground accordingly, tolerance enables us to respect, appreciate and accept the uniqueness of all people and treat them appropriately. Through understanding and open-mindedness, we attract those who are different and, by genuinely accepting and accommodating them, relationships blossom.

The seed of tolerance is love sown with compassion and care. Where there is a lack of love, there is a lack of tolerance.

The more loving we become, the more power there is in that love. For example, the bond of love between parents and children is such that the parents will tolerate anything to protect and care for them. At a time of need they do not worry about their own well-being and use the power of love to face all challenges. Love makes anything easier to tolerate.

Tolerance is first learned in the classroom of the family where we have to adjust to, and accommodate, the needs of others. School is the second classroom. Tests of tolerance are taken each and every day of our life. When we have the consciousness of appreciating the good in people and in the situation, we will more easily pass the tests. Any shade of disapproval will lead to lower marks. In order to pass with honour we need to use the power of tolerance as a protective shield so that our internal serenity remains untouched.

Discernment in Decision-Making

Tolerance is an inner strength, which enables us to face and transform misunderstandings and difficulties. We do this by using *discernment* in our decision-making. By delving into our conscience, we can determine what is right or wrong, what will bring benefit or loss to the self and others both in the short and long term.

The power of *discrimination* eliminates upheaval in our mind and intellect and between our emotions and reason. We are able to *respond* rather than *react* and there is neither conflict within the self nor with others, even if they insult us. Tolerance cultivates the ability to cool the strong and heated feelings of others.

Spiritual knowledge and insight allows us to stay content and unthreatened by people or circumstances. Keeping our mind and intellect clear and free from negative external vibrations which can cause doubt and discontent, we are able to see things as they really are, rather than how they appear to be, and take the necessary action.

When we are tolerant, we are like a tree with an abundance of fruits – even when pelted with sticks and stones, the tree gives its fruit in return.

The Ability to Accommodate

Certain circumstances often demand tolerance. Extremes of weather and varying levels of bodily pain are cases in point. Advances in technology, in the former, and medical treatment, in the latter, have reduced human discomfort greatly but not completely. At some level for all, tolerance becomes an indispensable power to cope.

Tolerance also develops our ability to accommodate the problems of everyday living such as traffic jams and cancelled trains. Through it we are able to let go, be light-hearted, make others light-hearted and move on in a calm way and inspire others to do likewise. Mountains are made into molehills and molehills are made into mustard seeds!

POINTS FOR REFLECTION

1. *What does 'tolerance' mean to you?*

2. *Think of someone who is an inspiring example of tolerance. What makes them so special? What are the secrets of their success?*

3. *In what ways do you demonstrate tolerance in your life?*

4. *Are there any areas in your life where you would like to be more tolerant? What discourages/prevents you from being more tolerant?*

5. *How can you develop greater tolerance power?*

UNITY

Do not follow the ideas of others, but learn to listen to the voice within yourself. Your body and mind will become clear and you will realise the unity of all things.
Dogen

Unity is harmony within and among individuals in a group. Unity is sustained by concentrating energy and focusing thought, by accepting and appreciating the value of the rich array of participants and the unique contribution each can make, and by remaining loyal not only to each other but also to the task.

Unity is all about union with other human beings. One of our basic needs is to feel a sense of belonging, to be part of a unified whole. We do not like being isolated, oblivious to the world outside. We are naturally sociable and curious about other people and cultures and feel a deep sense of compassion over the sufferings of, and injustices done, to others. We want to be together in natural gatherings like the family, or more structured organisations like the workplace, or a political party, which provide a common platform for us to talk and get to know, understand and help each other. This holds true for nations as well as individuals. Consciously, or unconsciously, we choose to be and act together.

Unity is created through a shared vision, a cherished hope, an altruistic aim, or a cause for the greater good. It enables us to reach beyond our own more limited needs and desires and gives us the sustenance, strength and courage to work together to make the impossible possible. Together with determination and commitment, unity makes the biggest task seem easy.

The greatness of unity is that everyone is respected. Unity creates the experience of co-operation, increases zeal and enthusiasm for the task and makes the atmosphere powerful and enabling.

The stability of unity comes from the spirit of equality and oneness, the noble values embodied in core universal principles.

In Harmony

The foundation of unity in any group is harmony both within and among the individuals in the group. For example, musicians need to practise playing their instrument alone before joining a symphony orchestra. In the same way, if we wish to play an effective part in a group, we need to spend time alone reflecting on the contribution we want to make (in terms of our capacity, potential, special talents, qualities, time and energy). For individual effectiveness, there needs to be clarity and cleanliness in our motives and intentions. Looking within helps to harmonise our thoughts, words and actions and enables us to adapt, as necessary, to the needs and aims of the group. Such personal integration keeps us 'in tune'.

Unity is sustained by:

❍ Concentrating our energy and focusing our thoughts on the goal;

❍ Accepting and appreciating the value of the rich array of the other participants and the unique contribution each can make;

❍ Remaining loyal to each other and the task.

With such a positive focus oneness in diversity is experienced and, because unity inspires stronger personal commitment and greater collective achievement, dance as well as music is attained.

Causes of Disunity

One note of disrespect can cause unity to be broken. Interrupting others, giving unconstructive and/or prolonged criticism, keeping watch over some, or trying to control others, are all strident chords, which strike harshly at our connections and relationships. Forms of ego such as dwelling on the weaknesses of others, gossip, hunger for recognition, jealousy, insecurity and doubt also undermine unity. Sometimes, even in little matters, we quickly get upset, aggressive, angry, or violent and may isolate ourselves in subgroups, producing dissension and conflict. Retuning and fine-tuning then become essential.

When brothers are seen as 'enemies', vital energy is misdirected and the home of unity shakes. Collectively, as a global family, we find it challenging to sustain unity against the common enemies of civil war, ethnic conflict, poverty, hunger and the violation of human rights.

Inner Focus

Creating unity in the world begins with a change in our individual consciousness. This requires our intellect to move away from conflict and confusion and, on an ongoing basis, to concentrate on restoring our inner strength and self-respect. Such inner focus does not isolate us but, in fact, brings us closer to others. In that closeness, in that shared humanity, there is the collective strength to pioneer and sustain fundamental and constructive transformation.

When we change, the world will change and peace and harmony will be restored.

POINTS FOR REFLECTION

1. *What does 'unity' mean to you?*

2. *Think of someone who is an inspiring example of unity. What makes them so special? What are the secrets of their success?*

3. *In what ways do you demonstrate unity in your life?*

4. *Are there any areas in your life where you would like more unity? What discourages/prevents you from practising greater unity?*

5. *How can you create more unity in your life?*

THINK ABOUT IT
Tools for Personal Change and Transformation

At this time in history, we are to take nothing personally, least of all, ourselves. For the moment that we do, our spiritual growth and journey comes to a halt.

The time of the lone wolf is over.

Gather yourselves!

Banish the word 'struggle' from your attitude and your vocabulary. All that we do now must be done in a sacred manner and in celebration.

We are the ones we have been waiting for.

Elders of the Hopi Nation

Tools for Personal Change and Transformation

Focusing on the individual, this section explains more fully some of the concepts covered in Section 1, describes some of the methods for positive change and offers tools for use both now and in the future.

The following observations, insights and exercises are all about enabling us to use the power of our mind to transform ourselves and really 'make it happen'.

There are so many ways to change our mind and make a real difference to the self and others. The choice is almost overwhelming and the danger is that we may end up using none of them!

To ensure this does not happen:

- Sit quietly by yourself;
- Turn your attention within;
- Ask your inner self, " Which technique do I need to practice at this moment in my life?";
- Experiment with it ;
- Keep using it until it becomes a habit;
- Move on to another technique.

Remember the Three 'A's

The three 'A's are: being *awake*, *aware* and paying *attention*. They are the foundation of inner peace and happiness and the keys to a successful, healthy life.

Being Awake

In India, they tell the story of Kumbhakarna. He was a giant who used to be awake for half the year and asleep for the other half. He lived near a town, which, one day, was attacked by an enemy army. The citizens did their best to repel the enemy but without success. They were in danger of being defeated. Their only hope lay with Kumbhakarna who was so big and strong that he could defeat any army. The people tried to wake him – they shook him, shouted at him, threw water over him. He would stir from his slumber, wake for a few moments and then return to sleep. This process of stirring, waking and then sleeping continued for some time until he finally realised what was going on, got his act together, and, with a roar, went off to defeat the army, much to the relief of the townspeople.

At this time we are rather like Kumbhakarna. We are living in a sleep of ignorance. Overwhelmed by the pleasures and pains of living in this materialistic world, many of us are no longer aware of our original spiritual identity and have lost touch with our inner powers and strengths, which, if realised, would enable us to rise up and defeat the chaos and negativity of a world which is a reflection of our own degraded consciousness.

Being Aware

To successfully 'wake up' we need to be *aware* of our spiritual identity and remember that each of us is a soul, separate from but connected to the body through which we interact with others and the world – like the driver of a bus, the captain of a ship, or the operator of a computer. This is something we have forgotten. Often we identify completely with, and spend much time and effort trying to satisfy, its unlimited demands.

The difference between being 'soul conscious' (awake) and 'body conscious' (asleep) is like the difference between day and night. The former is a state of being in which we feel powerful, positive, happy and content, the master of both the body and the mind. The latter eventually leads to feelings of distress, dissatisfaction, depression and despair as we become increasingly influenced by the spiritual dis-eases of anger, greed, strong physical desires, attachment and ego. Subconsciously we feel the pain of the contrast between the original and current state of the soul. We know deep inside that we have been and could be better than we are now but we do not know what to do about it.

Awareness of being a soul, and not just a body, is the foundation of raja yoga meditation as taught by the Brahma Kumaris. For more information see Appendix 1.

Paying Attention

As human beings in this troubled world, we need to 'wake up', become 'aware' of our inner qualities and strengths and then pay 'attention' as to how we are using our precious spiritual, mental, emotional and physical energies.

It is said that 'where the attention goes energy flows'. As spiritual beings, we need to be aware of where we are putting our attention or focus. Is it out of control? Does it flit from this to that? From positive to negative? From soul consciousness to body consciousness? For most of us the answer is "Yes" because like Khumbakarna, we keep falling asleep. One day we will fully awaken to our inner beauty, power and magnificence and, with the power of focus, perform wonders.

The key to being free and remaining awake, alert and aware is our thoughts.

EXPERIMENT

Spend a few minutes every day asking yourself "Who am I? In what ways am I more than a physical body?" Notice what answers come to your mind.

Turn Within

To 'turn within' means to become the observer of our thoughts and to reflect on our words and actions with a view to understanding the self and becoming more effective in our daily life.

When we align our thoughts, words and actions with the universal and divine principles that govern human nature and conduct, success and peace of mind is guaranteed because we are operating from a pure and positive place.

Turning within the self will uncover these principles – the unbreakable, enduring, fundamental truths that exist at the core of each human soul and transcend all belief systems. Qualities such as fairness and patience, honesty and integrity, benevolence and respect, accuracy and flexibility and all the divine virtues are part of our highest potential (see p.65). While we may practise these principles in varying degrees, there is universal agreement that such qualities do exist.

EXPERIMENT

Spend some time in solitude and think about the different qualities which you value. Remember times when you have used them in your life and get into the feelings associated with each one. You will be surprised at what you find!

Let Your Conscience be Your Guide

Every human being comes equipped with a conscience. It acts as a personal guide in applying and achieving the universal principles and is connected with the one universal Source of truth. It is important to 'tune in' to our conscience, feel its twinges, bites and other warning signs and listen when it talks.

When we conscientiously check and change the thoughts, words or actions that cause disservice to the self, or others, we become clean inside and out. This process takes courage and humility.

We also come equipped with the power of choice and free will. There is always more than one option we can take in any situation. Sitting in the driver's seat of the body (using the analogy of a car) we have the choice to go, stop, turn, give way, signal and so on.

Choosing to master our thoughts, words and actions is made easier with the roadmap of 'right' values and guiding principles. 'Right' values bring benefit to the self and others. They ensure safe driving and arrival at the proper destination. 'Wrong' values have harmful effects on the self and others and lead us astray. For example, the individual who places winning above all else, the organisation which places profit above customer safety, or the country that puts dogmatic ideals above human life, subscribe to 'wrong' values. Based on ulterior selfish motives such as greed, ego, or possessiveness, such values become major roadblocks or deep potholes. The results are sorrow, negativity, tension and conflict.

EXPERIMENT

Think of a time when you ignored your conscience.

What happened and how did you feel afterwards?

How can we 'sharpen up' our conscience and make it more effective?

Pay Attention to Your Intentions

Change begins in our individual consciousness and the intention behind our actions.

By taking personal responsibility for our thoughts, words and actions (using the analogy of driving a car) we are able to:

❍ Control the steering wheel of the mind and set in motion the process of change;

❍ Steer our thoughts in accurate and worthwhile directions;

❍ Apply the brake (i.e. put a full stop) to hurtful words before they are emitted;

❍ 'Pull over' to avoid 'hitting' someone else;

❍ Run the motor consistently to keep the battery charged using the power of pure actions performed without expectations.

When we pay attention to our motives and intentions, the engine runs clean and we experience greater mileage in terms of progress and performance.

Routine checking is also necessary. The differences between positive and negative intentions are subtle and sometimes difficult to detect. For example, the habit of seeing and speaking about the defects of others may, or may not, be part of our awareness as it is considered by many to be natural and 'normal'. Wanting to feel good at the expense of others lies at the heart of gossip. It has a direct, or indirect, effect, not only on the person spoken about but also on the gossipers and the general atmosphere.

Other forms of negative intentions include:

❍ Proving ourselves to be right by suppressing others;

❍ Manipulating people;

❍ Expecting respect without giving it;

❍ Trying to win the approval of others due to insecurity within.

While some motives may be obviously apparent to the self or others, some intentions may be hidden, even to the self, and require deep examination in order to be pinpointed, understood and changed.

Positive intentions, on the other hand, are recognised when we naturally and automatically:

❍ Give respect and benefit to others;

❍ See their uniqueness and qualities;

❍ Allow them to be themselves.

Even when we must say words which may be perceived as bitter medicine – as when giving feedback on inappropriate behaviour, or about something which may affect someone's life – the words are said directly and honestly, with humility and regard for the sensitivities of the other. When the recipient of feedback is treated with dignity and respect, listened to with empathy and involved in decisions about change, the discussion can be experienced as positive, opening doors to personal growth and change. Positive intentions encourage the giver of feedback to remain honest and 'up front', even when delivering a delicate message.

EXPERIMENT

Think of two situations – one where your intentions were 'pure' i.e. open, honest and beneficial and another when your real intentions were hidden and not so positive. Compare and contrast your feelings and the outcomes of the different intentions.

Create Quality Thoughts

If we were 'spotlessly clean' and able to utilise our power to create, sustain and destroy thoughts whenever we wished, whatever the circumstances, we would be the masters of our mind.

Through *self-awareness*, we can monitor the quality and direction of our thoughts; through *willpower*, we can apply a brake to undesirable thoughts (see *Break Negative Thought Patterns*). The extent to which we are able to apply the brake and steer the mind and intellect in worthwhile directions is the extent to which we are self-masters.

There are two reasons for 'accidents':

1. We forget that we are the driver and so lose control of the vehicle. In other words, our thoughts run away with us.

2. We fail to apply the brake fully. STOP MEANS 'STOP!' It does not mean inching forward with a few more wasteful thoughts. A full stop means to stop undesired thoughts. Period. Then, by shifting into a 'neutral' state of mind, we are in a better position to choose the direction, or lane, of new thoughts.

If each of us maintained a 'safe driving record' and took full responsibility for our driving etiquette, there would be countless better drivers and a much cleaner mental environment; thoughts of rubbish and dirt would not build up as sludge in our mind and travel would be simpler and more economical. Words of waste and negativity would not pollute the atmosphere. Actions that waste time and energy would be replaced by benevolent actions performed in the awareness of: "Whatever I do, others will see me and be inspired to do the same… Whatever I do, I will receive the return of that."

EXPERIMENT

Sit in solitude and spend time observing the quality of your thoughts.

Are they generally more 'positive' or 'negative'?

Notice the effect of each type of thought on your feelings and your body.

What effects do the different types of thoughts have on your behaviour?

What is the impact of the thoughts on your relationships?

How can you change your thoughts from 'negative' to 'positive'?

Remember the Law of Action and Reaction

The law of action and reaction, often known as the law of karma, states: 'For every action, there is an equal reaction'. In other words, what we sow, we reap – what we give out to the world and other people comes back in equal amount. If we give happiness, we will receive happiness in return. It is the same with sorrow. We can neither hide from, nor escape, the consequences of our actions. Sooner or later, the natural spiritual laws governing this universe expose the most secret act, punish every crime, reward every virtue and good act and redress every wrong in a subtle way but with absolute certainty and precision.

The law of karma is simple but, when understood deeply, it can provide useful insights and awaken us to the significance of each and every thought, word and action.

Karma begins in the mind as thoughts. Thoughts are the seeds of action. As is the thought, so is the result. Thoughts, like actions, spread vibrations and influence the atmosphere. Those vibrations are called subtle karmas.

Karma, both subtle and physical, returns vibrations, good or bad.

To understand the consequences of our attitude and deeds is to take total responsibility for our own state of mind and the quality of our actions. The law of karma puts us in the centre of our world. It helps us to understand that our current situation, whatever it might be, is the cumulative effect of our past actions. In other words, we have created the life we are now living and, as such, are responsible for it. We cannot blame anyone else. When we truly understand and accept this crucial spiritual law, however challenging it may at first appear, we are able to move from being a passive victim of life to being a master. We know we can create a better future for ourselves. This understanding lies at the heart of the 'law of attraction', which is currently so popular in the New Age movement.

By clearly defining the principle of cause and effect, the law of karma lays before us positive future directions of our own choice and making. Performing pure, beneficial actions will create that future. Having routine check-ups and changing for the better, guarantees safe arrival at the destination of our choice.

EXPERIMENT

Make a list of your achievements and successes and trace the link between your past actions and current position.

Think of one of the challenges you currently face in your life. Write a list of the lessons you are being taught.

What sort of future would you like and how are you going to create it?

Section 2

Break Negative Thought Patterns

Negative thoughts, include any form of criticising, complaining, comparing or blaming, as well as all the 'isms' such as sexism, racism, and nationalism. Such thoughts create tension and division and have harmful consequences for the self and others. They are reinforced by a set of negative beliefs and attitudes of which we are hardly aware – like a computer programme they run our reactions to life.

Knowing the difference between positive and negative thoughts and realising that we always have a choice about the thoughts we create, is the start of breaking these deeply engrained habitual patterns. It requires considerable self-awareness, willpower and a lot of practice to become the master of such thoughts.

EXPERIMENT

To change the pattern of your thinking remember S.O.S. – stand back, observe and, if necessary, steer your thoughts in another direction as follows:

1) STAND BACK FROM YOUR THOUGHTS. Withdraw. View your thoughts as a 'detached observer' without judgement, criticism or blame.

2) OBSERVE AND EVALUATE EACH THOUGHT as it flashes across the screen of your mind. Check the quality and direction. Notice which thoughts make you feel good and those that make you feel bad.

3) STEER YOUR THOUGHTS. Create powerful, peaceful, inspiring useful thoughts that will bring benefit to yourself and others.

Be gentle on yourself. If old thought patterns and negative past experiences creep into your mind, recognize them as you would a red light. Then, simply apply the brake and come to a FULL STOP! That means stop thinking about them and change direction. Replace them with something better.

Take Time Out

The power to control our thoughts is the key to a better life.

Thoughts are more powerful than a rocket. In less than one second, we can go wherever we want, experience closeness to anyone, or adopt whatever state of mind we wish.

Using thoughts in a worthwhile way creates good moods, mindsets or actions. Such thoughts are created more easily when we truly recognise our own self-worth and the worth of others.

To make the most of our thought power we need to take time out, sit in solitude and create a peaceful space in the mind where we can:

- *Plan* for the self (short and long-term) and others (community or other service activities):
- *Churn* or think about the learning points made, for example, at a conference or lecture or in a quality book;
- *Check* the self with an honest heart, including examining our intentions; then change inaccuracies or weaknesses – first in thought as a way to rehearse the improvement before putting it into action;
- *Visualise* ways to incorporate values, virtues, or powers into our daily activity.

Knowing what we need to do, we must put it into practice and change the habits that control our life.

EXPERIMENT

When you first wake up spend 10 minutes preparing yourself mentally for the day. See yourself as having a great day – really look forward to it. See everything as an exciting opportunity to learn and grow.

In the evening spend another 10 minutes reviewing the day and the lessons learned. Notice what worked and what could have been better. Then let go of the day and go to bed looking forward to the next day.

Put an End to Wasteful Thinking

The signs of wasteful thoughts are feelings of distress, loss of happiness or pleasure, a mind filled with confusion and/or an inability to make accurate decisions.

For example, it is not a good use of time to continuously think about a past action that we regret. Better to;

○ Learn from the situation,

○ Make amends if you can, and

○ Move on.

Self transformation can happen the moment there is *realisation* and *reconciliation*.

EXPERIMENT

Think of someone you dislike. Write down the reasons why you dislike them and then make a list of their good points. Remember these good points the next time you see them and notice the difference it makes to the relationship.

Remember, where the attention goes energy flows.

Remember 'Not' and 'Dot'

When any circumstances arise which cause havoc with our emotions – and we want to stop thinking about it but can't – we can try the following.

EXPERIMENT

Think "'Not' means 'Stop'". Then apply a 'dot'… a FULL STOP! Not a question mark, or an exclamation mark, or a comma but a FULL STOP! Simply refuse to think about it anymore. That will automatically defuse the charged emotions and make the situation become 'not'.

Don't Ask "Why?", Simply Fly!

Question marks are the most difficult to stop. Our minds often race with questions such as, "Why did this happen? Why didn't I say, or do that? Why did that person do that?"

The way to manage thoughts of "Why?" is to fly. We make the mind light by directing our consciousness to a higher place, for example, to the top of the tallest building in our city, or to a cloud in the sky, and observe the circumstance from that place.

By 'flying away' or detaching in this way, we change our perspective. In this detached, yet alert, state of mind, we are better able to see what is right or wrong, or what should or should not happen. We are then able to *respond* and perform actions based on our innermost values rather than *react* under the pressure of external circumstances.

EXPERIMENT

Think of a situation that you are finding challenging. Fly up above and see the scene from a distance and get a new, detached perspective on it. Ask yourself, "How can I deal with the situation in a more positive and productive way?"

Generate Pure Thoughts and Good Wishes

There is increasing evidence to suggest that the thoughts of human beings are very powerful. Like other forms of energy, they can be used in a constructive, or destructive, way to make life on earth a living heaven, or hell.

For many people, negative thinking is so normal that it is as natural as breathing. It is accepted as part of the human condition. The results of such unexamined thinking can be seen all around us in the form of racism, sexism, nationalism, homophobia and all the other prejudices that fuel so much anger, conflict and strife in the world.

Positive thoughts are more powerful – they can reduce the crime rate in cities, alter the crystalline structure of water, heal people and even affect our genes! All the good things in life start from a powerful, positive thought.

Silently sending pure thoughts and good wishes to another is a very effective way to communicate. Such thoughts benefit both the sender and receiver and create a powerful atmosphere.

Pure thoughts and good wishes can be sent to individuals, groups, countries in distress, nature, the world and so on. Such a form of communication is a good habit to cultivate and is especially powerful when the thoughts are backed up with beneficial words and worthwhile activities e.g. sending loving and healing thoughts to a country affected by a natural disaster and then raising funds to help pay for food and shelter.

EXPERIMENT

Spend a few minutes sending out good wishes to someone you find challenging in your life. Notice the difference it makes to you and your relationship with that person over time.

Develop an Attitude of Gratitude

All of us have an attitude towards the self, others and the world. Attitude is like a filter, or a pair of glasses, which colours the way we see things. It is an approach to life, which predetermines the way that we will respond or react in any situation. Generally speaking, our attitude is either positive and life-affirming or negative and life-denying; either we see the world as a place of adventure, wonder, beauty, learning and abundance, or a place of darkness, danger, fear and scarcity. What we see is what we get and our energy levels and vibrations will respond accordingly. A positive attitude makes us feel great – we are full of enthusiasm and are inspired to give of our best. A negative attitude drains our energy and leaves us feeling depleted, distressed and/or depressed.

A quick and easy way to shift our attitude from negative to positive is to develop an 'attitude of gratitude' and count our many blessings rather than take things for granted or complain about the things we want but have not got.

EXPERIMENT

For one week write a list every day of 50 things that you are grateful for. For example, being able to walk, or talk, having friends or family, the sunshine, the rain, the air we breathe. There are so many things to be grateful for that you will not want to stop writing!

Believe and Achieve

Beliefs are like the basic programme in a computer. They are a form of conditioning that help us to make sense of the world and constantly affect the way we perceive and interact with it. They are so deeply embedded in our sub conscious mind that we are not aware of them and do not challenge or question them until faced by the sorrow they sometimes cause.

Throughout the course of our life, especially when we were young and in awe of adults, whether parents, relatives, teachers or religious leaders, we have absorbed so many inaccurate beliefs about ourselves, others and the world. For example, we may believe that we are 'stupid' or 'unworthy' or do not deserve the best in life, that other people cannot be trusted, that happiness never lasts and that life is full of conflict and suffering. Such beliefs are like the bars of a cage – they prevent us from growing; they stunt our ambition and encourage passivity and alienation. We become the victims of our own life and hand over our power to others, hoping for something (like winning the lottery) or someone (like a wonderful partner) to change our lives and make us happy.

If we wish to be the master of our life and enjoy it to the full, we need to become aware of, and root out, the old damaging beliefs that hold us back and replace them with insights that are more in line with our inner strengths, qualities, talents, skills and values. Each of us has unlimited potential and the ability to create for ourselves a wonderful life of love and happiness. It may take time and a lot of effort but it can be done provided we have faith in ourselves and are determined to make it a reality.

EXPERIMENT

Write down what you would love to do with your life if you had enough money and time.

What is your secret dream or passion?

Make a list of the beliefs that are holding you back from achieving your dream. Replace them with beliefs that will give you the inspiration and motivation to make your dreams come true.

Appreciate Rather than Denigrate

We all like to be loved, valued and approved of by others rather than criticised, humiliated and rejected, in the same way that plants prefer water and sunshine, rather than dryness and cold draughts. We flourish in an atmosphere of encouragement, respect and positivity, where our talents and contribution are acknowledged and appreciated. Yet, surprisingly, many of us do not experience this in our daily life, whether at work or at home. Our efforts are often taken for granted and attention is drawn to our mistakes and failures to live up to the expectations of others. Often the words "please", "thank you" and "well done" are in short supply.

Appreciation is a powerful tool for personal and social change and it starts with me. If I want more appreciation in my life, I need to give it first – to myself, my partner, parents, children and grandchildren, friends and colleagues, those who serve me in the shops and even strangers on the street. The more I appreciate the daily acts of kindness and consideration of other people, the more they will appreciate mine. Together we can create a feeling of co-operation, community and harmony wherever we are.

EXPERIMENT

Make a habit of saying "please", "thank you" and "well done" whenever you can and notice the difference it makes.

Have Pure Vision for the Self and Others

How do we see ourselves and other people? Is it with dislike and distaste? Or with love and regard? Do we hold on to past mistakes – the things we, or others, have said or done that have hurt us? Do we notice only weaknesses, rather strengths?

There is a saying 'If you spot it, you have got it.' In other words, people are a mirror for us and we only see in them what is in our own self. If we think someone is full of ego, mean or aggressive, it is because those states resonate with our own state. This realisation is quite painful but, once accepted, it is most helpful as we begin to see everyone as our teacher and so eliminate much of the conflict and tension, rejection and anger in our life.

One of the secrets of a successful life is to 'see but not see' and 'hear but not hear' and maintain a very positive and powerful vision of the person before us. If we focus our attention on their original, true character and potential rather than their stress, confusion or anger, we will both empower and encourage that person and, at the same time, deepen our own acceptance, compassion and love for all humanity and ourselves.

EXPERIMENT

Write an honest list of all your 'good' and 'bad' points. Which list is longer? If the latter is longer than the former you are likely to suffer from a lack of self-esteem and confidence. How can you turn your weaknesses into strengths?

Influence the Atmosphere

As human beings we are very sensitive to the atmosphere around us. We can walk into a room where there has been an argument and immediately feel the tension in the air, even though no one may say anything. Likewise, we can appreciate the peaceful, calm space of a church, temple, mosque or meditation room.

A negative atmosphere can influence us, or we can choose to influence it. Modelling virtues, exercising powers and letting our innermost values guide us is the way to create a positive atmosphere wherever we go

EXPERIMENT

The next time you go into what feels like a negative atmosphere see if you can change it using some of the methods suggested in this book.

Practise Divine Virtues

Divine virtues are qualities and/or values in action, which are universally recognised as intrinsically good. They include the following:

○ Accuracy	○ Happiness	○ Responsibility
○ Benevolence	○ Honesty	○ Royalty
○ Carefree	○ Humility	○ Self-confidence
○ Cheerful	○ Introversion	○ Serenity
○ Cleanliness	○ Liberty	○ Simplicity
○ Contentment	○ Lightness	○ Stability
○ Cooperation	○ Love	○ Surrender
○ Courage	○ Loyalty	○ Sweetness
○ Detachment	○ Maturity	○ Tirelessness
○ Determination	○ Mercy	○ Tolerance
○ Discipline	○ Obedience	○ Trust
○ Fearlessness	○ Patience	○ Truthfulness
○ Flexibility	○ Peacefulness	○ Unity
○ Generosity	○ Purity	○ Wisdom
○ Gentleness	○ Respect	

All these inspiring virtues are to be found within each human being. The more we water them with our attention and put them into practice, the more they will grow and the happier we will become. Challenges will come to test our virtues. Be grateful for the tests. Without them how could we learn, develop inner strength and fulfil our true potential?

EXPERIMENT

Choose a virtue. Spend time in silence thinking about it and feeling it. Then practise it for two days.

If you are facing a challenging situation, rather than worry about it or react to it, choose a virtue that you think will make a difference and follow the exercise above.

Section 2

Be Power-Packed and Powerful

Powers, virtues and values are strongly interconnected and support each other throughout the 'drama' of our life.

Power gives us the ability to put things into action.

Values are the original core qualities of the inner self – peace, love, happiness, wisdom/truth and purity.

Virtues are the expression of our qualities and values in action through our thoughts, words and deeds.

One leading power, for instance, automatically calls into action other supporting powers or virtues. Underlying values are like the 'backstage crew', and are on hand to offer assistance.

The following powers are very useful.

The Power to Accommodate: This is the ability to adjust to people or situations, be unaffected by the atmosphere and perceive exactly what is required rather than try to impose our will.

The Power to Discern: This power helps us to distinguish between 'real' and 'apparent' truth, between things of temporary and eternal value and also the superficial and the subtle. It helps us to recognise and resist traps of illusion, however sweetly decorated and enticing, see through disguises and act confidently and wisely for the greater good.

The Power to Face: This power gives us the courage and confidence to deal with any person, or situation. Nothing appears as an obstacle and challenges are perceived as stepping-stones to learning the deeper lessons of life. It helps us to conquer all types of fear, insecurity and doubt, especially about ourselves.

The Power to Judge: This power helps us assess any situation in a detached and impartial way, with clarity and precision, and take appropriate action based on respect and good wishes for all those involved.

The Power to Pack Up: This is the ability to set aside all wasteful thoughts in one second so that there is lightness and freedom from burdens and worries. Though we may have many responsibilities, we cease to equate them with worry. By going deep into the self, our preoccupation with the limited external activities of the past, present, or future are 'packed up' for that limited time period and we experience an unlimited consciousness, which puts things in perspective.

The Power to Withdraw: This is the ability to detach the mind from a situation and, with full awareness, observe the scene like a director and think and act in ways that do not disturb our peace of mind.

EXPERIMENT

Think of a challenging situation in your life and consider which of the above powers would help you deal with the situation most effectively. Practise it for at least 21 days (that is how long it takes to change a habit) and see what happens.

SECTION 3

MAKING IT HAPPEN

Workshops and Activities for Collective Change

We must become the change we want to see.

Mahatma Gandhi

Workshops and Activities for Collective Change

Introduction

Since values should be explored and understood as well as lived and experienced, this series of workshops helps participants discover how they can apply practically the core values, which help guide our daily activities. Designed by a variety of professionals, they have been developed for:

○ Global forums;

○ Organisations, businesses and healthcare settings;

○ Communities and a broad range of other civic and social settings;

○ Families in a structured learning environment;

○ Elementary, middle and secondary schools.

With the exception of the classroom curriculum which obviously requires a teacher, the workshops call for a group leader, or facilitator. An experienced facilitator will be able to present the material easily. Given the level of detail included in the design, even inexperienced people, with support and encouragement, will be able to run the workshops if they have the interest and want to become instruments for making positive things happen. The effort, care and preparation it takes to facilitate a workshop is usually recognised and appreciated by the participants and the personal benefits for the facilitator are limitless.

The Role of the Facilitator

The role of a facilitator is to help create a safe and secure space and learning environment, which ensures a positive experience for each participant.

An effective group facilitator demonstrates the following behaviours:

1. Manages the times of the session.

Section 3

2. Keeps the group on track and on target.

3. Ensures a good balance between structure and 'going with the flow' of the group.

4. Respects and supports each group member.

5. Stays 'neutral'. Accepts what is being said without value judgment or playing the 'expert'.

6. Is sensitive to the feelings of group members, e.g. recognising clues provided by non-verbal signs such as when the group is restless and in need of a 5-minute break.

7. Encourages, in a non-threatening way, quieter people to share. For example, "Some of you quieter folks must have thoughts about that," or "Joan and Juan have been sharing a lot of interesting thoughts. What about those of you who have not offered your thoughts yet?"

8. Uses silence in an effective way, e.g. allows participants enough time to form a response to a question, or provides enough time for silent reflection.

Ground Rules

To ensure that group sessions are effective, facilitators may want to introduce some 'ground rules' or have participants suggest their own ground rules, which then become the group's norms. Some examples include:

1. Start and end on time.

2. Participate actively.

3. Listen and understand.

4. Be honest and open.

5. Build on each other's ideas.

6. No idea is a bad idea.

7. Leave 'baggage' outside.

8. Be non-violent – no 'killer' phrases.

9. Respect confidentiality and build trust.

10. Adopt a team approach.

Have fun!

INDIVIDUALS

INNER LEADERSHIP WORKSHOP [1]

Introduction

In the present pressure-driven world there is an increasing demand not only for efficiency and timeliness in our dealings with the world, but for more emotional sensitivity in our relationships. Both of these life supports are only possible if we have command over ourselves from within.

We have two lives – the one we live and the one we could live if we were only able to understand how to liberate the potential of the values and strengths that reside inside us. We have to be able to live not only the length of our lives but its breadth also. There is so much more than just living on automatic pilot, going from one day to the next, from one situation to the next, impelled by circumstance and obligation. Real and lasting change does not come from quick-fix recipes but from a deep sense of purpose and the self-discipline necessary to give that purpose direction.

The subject of leadership has been flouted and exploited to a huge extent in the modern world. The subjects related to inner leadership and the possibilities that it opens up have been less so. It stands to reason that if we really want to be able to lead others, we first have to be able to lead ourselves. We cannot demand from others what we ourselves are not prepared to do and show.

The questions of "What?", "Why?", "How to?" and "Where to?" are the subjects of this Inner Leadership Workshop.

---

1 Designed by Ken O'Donnell, a specialist in quality management and organisational development based in Brazil.

Section 3

Aim/Objective

The main objective is to help people to understand the basis of a life filled with more joy and discovery. It will help the participants to have a greater sense of identity, purpose and direction and to begin the process of breaking free from whatever is holding them back.

Who is it For?

The subject matter and the exercises can be used individually, or can be facilitated in groups of up to 30 people. It is for those who are looking for clarification about how to begin putting their lives into a positive direction and creating a better future for themselves and consequently for the people around them.

Duration

The workshop has been organised in three parts of around 90-120 minutes each (depending on the depth that you want reach) so it can be comfortably arranged into a half-day format. As the workshop is of an introductory nature, it can lead or inspire participants to go deeper into these topics at their own leisure.

Workshop Structure

Each workshop has the following four interwoven aspects:

- ○ Instructions for facilitators (if you are doing this workshop as an individual you can skip these instructions);
- ○ Brief explanation of concepts with the relevant illustrations;
- ○ Exercises, which can be copied into a notebook;
- ○ Reflections.

INNER LEADERSHIP WORKSHOP

Part 1: Sense of Identity (Who Am I?)
(90-120 minutes)

1.1 Introduction

Introduce yourself. Introduce the workshop, briefly, as being ideal for people looking for clarification of their way forward and a better understanding of themselves. Ask the participants to choose a partner and for each to interview the other. Ask them to:

○ Introduce themselves;

○ Share a very positive experience they have had over the last 12 months;

○ Share it with the wider group.

The purpose of this is to allow the participants to become comfortable in talking to each other.

Talk the participants quickly through the sequence. Explain that you will go into the detail of each section at the appropriate time.

○ Part 1. Who am I?

○ Part 2. Purpose – What do I really want to be and do?

○ Part 3. Direction – Where do I want to go?

1.2 Being the Detached Observer

Explain the concept of being a detached observer and that during this workshop their evaluations need to be done while in this mental state. We need to be outside the issue not inside it. This means that we maintain a separation from the things we are thinking about to enable us to be free from any emotional pulls we might otherwise have. Being a detached observer is a powerful mental state to adopt whenever we are deciding major issues. It enables thinking to be clearer and more insightful than otherwise. It is simply true that if we are inside a situation (and emotionally involved) it is much harder to see all the issues and perspectives than if we are looking at it from the outside.

1.3 Keeping Focus in the Chaos

Explain how having a sense of identity gives us strength of character compared with allowing ourselves to be pushed and pulled by the role that we might identify with at the time. For example, a mother would be feeling good if her child is being praised at school and winning prizes on the sports field. However, she probably would not feel so good if her child was behaving badly at school, causing mischief and getting into trouble. A sense of true identity means that we can choose how we feel.

There are two paradigms here:

1. What is happening around us, and
2. How we feel about it (identification with role).

How do I want to feel today? What is happening around me? (clear sense of identity and control of emotions – able to be the detached observer easily).

Having a sense of identity makes it easier to understand or identify our sense of purpose, from which it is easier to see our sense of direction. When these three aspects – the sense of identity, purpose and direction – are clear they become like anchors to keep us stable in all situations, even the most turbulent, since our way forward will always become clear as the diagram shows:

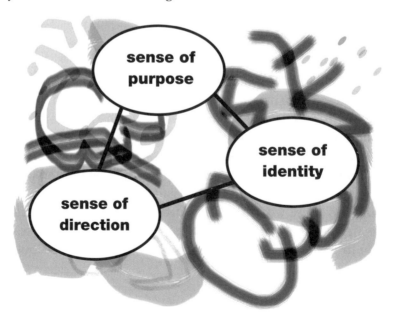

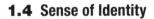

1.4 Sense of Identity

Explain how people often think of their identity as being defined by their roles in life, for example their job, house, family, connections and the like. However, the deeper identity is much more connected with the actor behind those roles, called by some as the spirit within. It is this spiritual actor who is the source of:

○ The behaviour in each set of circumstances;

○ The choices we make;

○ The values we think are important;

○ The relationships we create.

1.5 Clues from My Last 12 Months

Invite the participants to look back over the last 12 months and pick the high points and low points of their lives that they can identify. Keep it to just 4–5 of each. Even if they have just been sitting at home, there are lessons for them to learn. *For each point, they need to think out what is the main lesson or learning they have gained from that experience.*

It is important for the participants to be very honest with themselves. They need to adopt the state of being a detached observer while doing this work.

Some soft music will help them think more deeply.

Some examples would be:

High points	Main learning	Low points	Main learning
I visited China	I opened my mind to other cultures	I had a huge argument with my son	Harmony at home is very important to me
I finally finished building my house	It's good to use my hands and not only my head	I stopped practising meditation because of lack of time	I can't live without God
I changed my job	I need more self-confidence	I lied to my boss	Lying lowers my self-respect
I resolved a conflict with a person who is important to me	She has more virtues than defects	I badly damaged my new car	I need to be less attached
I finished a very complex report	Patience and determination are a great help to me	My wallet was stolen with my ID and credit cards	I need to be more careful

The participants can copy a blank table in their notebook and work on their own examples.

1.6 My Strengths

Invite the participants to look at the things they have been doing over the last 12 months and to pick out the type of things that have brought benefit to others, that they are good at, or that they particularly like doing.

This exercise will give them a better insight as to what their purpose is which they will do later.

On a blank sheet of paper write the answers to this question:

What am I good at, or particularly like doing, that benefits others?

1.7 Clues from My Relationships

Life is based on relationships. The quality of our lives is defined by the quality of our relationships. The quality of our relationships is based on our perception of them and experience in them. This, in turn, is based on our interaction with others. If we have no interaction with others then there is no relationship. To improve the quality of our interaction it is fundamentally important to understand what we can really give to a relationship, or to others, and what we receive from the relationship, or others. Emphasise that it is the positive aspects that are being looked for. Look at the following diagram:

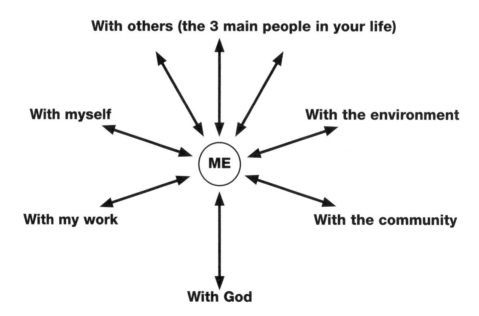

The participants can copy this diagram in their notebook. Ask them to become the detached observer and identify what they *give positively* in each relationship and what they *take positively* from each relationship.

You can play quiet music while they reflect on the giving and taking that happens in each relationship. The participants can write a word or a phrase, on each side of the arrow, that represents the giving and taking.

1.8 My Advice to Myself

Invite the participants to continue in the state of a detached observer and to respond to these questions:

1. Why do I live my life the way that I do?

2. Can I live my life in a better way?

3. To live my life more effectively, what are the three main pieces of advice I can give to myself, looking at my last 12 months? Use the verb in the imperative (e.g. I must...).

For example:

O I must have more faith in myself.

O I must learn to smile more.

O I must see only the virtues in others and not the defects.

1.9 Reflection

Sit comfortably and gradually let your awareness become one of detached observation. Imagine that you are sitting in the last row in the theatre from which you can see your life being acted out on the stage. You can see the last year with all of its ups and downs pass before you. You remember the lessons that you have learned. You remember that you are the actor and not the roles, that you are a spiritual being having a human experience and not just a human being looking for a spiritual experience. In this state you see how your relationships are formed around you because of the way you think and act. You realise that you do have specific strengths within you that can be brought into play whenever you so choose. You remember the main advice that you have given to yourself and feel that yes, it is possible to proceed in that way.

Section 3

INNER LEADERSHIP WORKSHOP

Part 2: Sense of Purpose (What Do I Really Want to Be and Do?) *(90–120 minutes)*

2.1 The Role of Beliefs in Our Lives

One of the main blocks to living a deeper sense of purpose are the beliefs that we have about ourselves and others.

Invite the participants to discuss the question of how much what we believe about ourselves, others and the world in which we live affects the way we do things and interact with others.

They should be able to conclude that our beliefs dominate every area of our lives. Everything we perceive in the world about us is filtered through our belief systems. For example, if I believe I am an important person and, therefore, not to be taken lightly, then I will feel insults strongly. If I have self-respect, I will not be concerned about insults (though I may recognise them for what they are).

An ancient Chinese story tells how a man lost an axe. He believed his neighbour had stolen his axe so he locked up everything he had and was unfriendly to his neighbour (without knowing for sure if he was guilty or not). When he found the axe again, his neighbour seemed quite different.

If I think the world is a dangerous place, I will live in fear and keep a distance from everyone.

Ask the participants to give their own examples.

2.2 Limiting Beliefs

Explain the following examples. It is a description of recurring patterns that have probably been evident over the last 12 months. It refers to how we make excuses to explain our limitations. The limitations are mostly self-imposed and, therefore, they have to be broken down by ourselves. Invite the participants to look at the state of their relationships over the last 12 months and fill in the table in their workbooks responding to the questions:

○ How do I limit myself?

○ What do I say to myself to explain these limitations?

Here are some examples:

How do I limit myself?	What do I say to myself to explain these limitations?
I always achieve as much as I possibly can	How can anybody do more than that?
I always see the defects of other people before seeing their virtues	Everyone is selfish and only looks to their own interests. Why shouldn't I?
I do things to please others whose attention I want	I need the recognition of my colleagues
I always start projects well but I never finish them	I don't have enough time

The participants can copy a blank table into their notebooks and work on their own examples.

2.3 My Foundational Beliefs

Using the results from the previous exercise, invite the participants into an introspective state to identify their principal limiting belief and how it could be revised in the form of a new foundational belief, to lead to a better life. The results should go into their notebook. For example:

Limiting belief:	A new base belief for a better life
I can never be a good cook	I can do anything I want if I give myself enough time.
I don't have faith in my own success	I already have within me everything I need for success

2.4 The Main Virtues I Have

Look at the following list of the virtues:

Accepting	Confident	Discreete	Hospitable	Moderate	Self-controlled	Tender
Accurate	Considerate	Economical	Humble	Noble	Self-disciplined	Tireless
Adaptable	Contented	Empathetic	Idealistic	Nonviolent	Sensitive	Tolerant
Authentic	Cooperative	Energetic	Innocent	Obedient	Serene	Tough
Balanced	Courageous	Enthusiastic	Integrity	Open	Serviceable	Tranquil
Benevolent	Courteous	Faithful	Introspective	Optimistic	Silent	Trusting
Brave	Creative	Firm	Joyous	Organised	Simple	Trustworthy
Carefree	Dedicated	Flexible	Just	Patient	Sincere	Truthful
Caring	Detached	Focused	Kind	Peaceful	Sober	Unified
Cautious	Determined	Forgiving	Liberal	Perseverance	Spontaneous	Vision

Cheerful	Dignified	Friendly	Light	Prudent	Stable	Vitality
Clean	Diligent	Generous	Loving	Pure	Strong	Willpower
Committed	Diplomatic	Grateful	Loyal	Respectful	Surrendered	Wise
Communication	Direct	Honest	Mature	Responsible	Sweet	Zealous
Compassionate	Discerning	Honourable	Merciful	Selfless	Tactful	

Ask the participants to review the list of virtues and choose which **four** virtues they have used most over the last 12 months and write them in their notebook according to the following pyramid diagram.

Get them to pick just **three** virtues that they used in their work and other activities and to write those in. Then repeat this for **two** virtues they used most in their relationships.

Finally, ask them to look at the **nine** virtues they have written down and choose their **main** virtue (that has most significance for them at this time) and to write that down. When they have done this, and if there is time, they can share their discovered virtues with another participant.

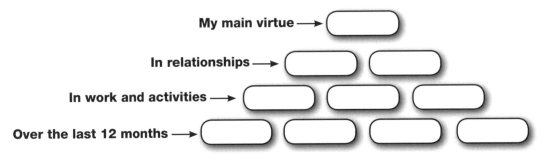

2.5 Virtues and Purpose

Tell the participants that purpose is the expression of our deepest virtues. For example, when you see a street lamp, its whole structure is involved in its function of shining light. It has been made for exactly that reason. In the same way, virtues provide our inner structure. They have a lot to do with what we are supposed to be doing in this world. When we are able to express what we are internally then we feel light and happy. Invite the participants to discuss the idea that when we are being who we really are, we feel happy.

They should arrive at the idea that when we are living our purpose, life just flows for us. Everything you need to fulfil your purpose will arrive for you at the right time. Ask them to give examples of how they were when they felt that 'the universe was conspiring' in their favour.

2.6 Discovering My Purpose

Invite the participants to talk in pairs about these questions:

○ If you had real freedom to really do what you want, or to be your true self, what would you be doing?

○ In what field would you be expressing that?

○ Who with (if with anyone)?

Ask them to take their answers into consideration when filling in the following blanks:

I will use my (virtue) to _____.

They need to fill in the blanks as in the following examples:

○ I will use my capacity to network to enable me to serve as a bridge between underprivileged young people and the wider community.

○ I will use my ability to communicate to teach people how to live better and be happier.

○ I will use my loving and caring nature to raise my children to be fine adults.

2.7 Reflection

Sit comfortably and gradually let your awareness become one of detached observation and again see your life being acted out on the stage. Again look at the beliefs that have been shaping your life and especially the reasons why you have been limiting your own progress. Hold up your new foundational beliefs and feel their importance. Go through each of the 10 virtues one by one in the pyramid that you have drawn and experience how they reflect who you really are in this world. Dwell especially on the virtue that you have identified as your main one. Look at the phrase that has translated those virtues into some practical field of action and which you have written down as your purpose. Send your mind into the future and see where that sense of purpose points.

Section 3

INNER LEADERSHIP WORKSHOP

Part 3: Sense of Direction (Where Do I Want to Go?) *(90–120 minutes)*

3.1 Purpose and Self-Progress

Draw 3 overlapping circles on the whiteboard and label them *Inner State*, *Serving Others* and *Relationships*.

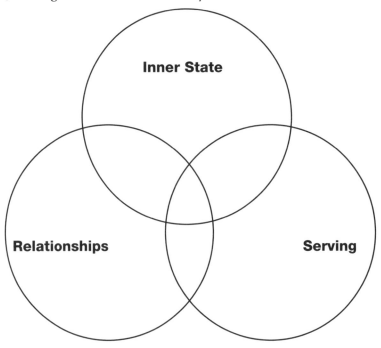

Explain that this diagram shows how self-progress is a result of the balance between the inner state, relationships and the service that we perform for others and for the world. This balance is essential in order to retain a sense of happiness and keep on course no matter what the odds.

The inner state is the result of all the adjustments that we make internally while we are living out our lives. It is a mixture of understanding, experience and power. When we are living according to our purpose, our inner state becomes tranquil and content.

The quality of our relationships, as we have already seen, depends on the expression of our virtues. Virtues can be seen as 'shock absorbers' in the relationships. The difference between driving along a road that is full of holes, with or without suspension, is easy to understand. Others can be as they are, with their specific mix of virtues and defects, but in order to keep relationships healthy we need to consciously practise virtues.

The field of serving others is definitely where we see the expression of our sense of purpose. *To serve others and to serve the world is probably the most pure expression of what is best in us.*

If progress in the inner state is indicated by tranquillity and contentment, progress in relationships is indicated by ease, harmony and co-operation. This leads to the creation of opportunities for service as well as the means to serve those opportunities

3.2 Draw a Symbol of your Purpose

Ask the participants to draw a symbol or icon that represents their purpose from Part 2.6 on a blank sheet of paper. Give some examples – hands, a star, a butterfly, a sun, a tree, a river coming into an ocean, an arrow hitting a target and so on. Stimulate creativity as much as possible.

3.3 Envision the Expression of your Purpose

Invite the participants to consider:

If I live my life according to my purpose, how will it express itself in terms of my inner state, relationships and service over the next two years?

They can do this work according to the following table. Their vision for these three aspects should be expressed in as much detail as possible.

Aspect	How will I be in 2 years time?
Inner State	
Relationships	
Serving others	

3.4 Tasks for the Next 30 Days

Ask the participants to study their previous table and to consider the immediate tasks they will need to carry out to get themselves headed in the direction of their purpose.

THERE IS NOTHING AS POWERFUL AS TAKING ACTION. If all of the previous work in this workshop is not converted into immediate action, the momentum for self-change will be lost.

They can use the following table as an example:

Direction	Related tasks for the next 30 days
Spend more quality time with my family	• Talk with my wife today to fix some time together next weekend • Involve the family with the planning of a weekend away over next Easter
Learn meditation	• Look up the workshops that are available • Go to the local bookshop to see related books
Do a post-grad workshop on 'Quality of Life in the Workplace'	• Do a web search on related workshops in my town • Make adjustments to my agenda for the second semester
Loose 5 kilos by July	• Visit the gym on X-street to check out what they offer • Do a web search on diet today
Finally write the book on 'Conflict Resolution'	• Gather all the material that I have on this subject by Sunday • Call my contact at the publishing house to fix a meeting

3.5 Reflection

Go to a place behind your eyes and observe the panorama of your life, the past and its significance in bringing you to the present and the realisations you are now having in shaping your future choices, decisions and actions.

Meditate for some moments on the symbol that you have drawn to represent your purpose and consider each of the main aspects of your own progress, how you want the progress with regard to your inner state, your relationships and the service that you can do with others to truly reflect your sense of purpose. Consider the basic directions that are within each of these areas and look at the tasks that you have written down. They are not just mere actions but they are the springboard for the changes that you need to bring in your life.

ORGANISATIONS

VALUES WORKSHOPS FOR PROFESSIONALS[1]

Introduction

This series of creative workshops can be presented separately, or combined, to form a course in values development. Participants define and reflect on values within the self, in their relationships and in the organisation. Lively large and small-group exercises focus on values of the past, present and future and engender a spirit of oneness and commonality among the participants as they join together to find ways to live the values in a professional setting.

Target Audience: Professionals from management and non-management ranks, from large and small corporations and businesses, from the public, private, or social sectors.

Duration: One day, or a series of one- or two-hour modules.

Methodology: Interactive lecture, large- and small-group discussion, creative small-group exercises, personal reflection.

Subject Matter: Understanding and defining values, creative values, organisational values, integration of values, values in relationships, re-defining values, building on the Values Statements in this book.

Materials: Easels, flipchart paper, masking tape, markers, lined writing paper, pencils, and copies of specific Value Statements from this book.

---

1 Created by Mike George, an international management consultant, spiritual teacher and best-selling author based in the UK

1. UNDERSTANDING AND DEFINING VALUES
(75–90 minutes)

Purpose: To set the stage for a warm and friendly session; to provide time for silent introspection as well as interaction with others; to discuss values, particularly organisational values, in a constructive format.

Objective: For participants to become aware of and understand the meaning and importance of values.

Method

1.1 Introduce yourself providing brief background:

- ○ Ask participants to give their introduction including: name, where from, and 'what you valued as a child'.
- ○ Begin the round by sharing what you valued as a child. *(5 minutes)*

1.2 Set the context of values in the world today, including interactive discussion around the following issues: *(5 minutes)*

- ○ Absence/disappearance of values today;
- ○ How important values are in directing human behaviour;
- ○ The need for a restoration of values today.

1.3 Guide the participants through the following series of questions and discussions:

a) *What are the main factors which influence your values in any given situation?*

- ○ Personal reflection. *(5 minutes)*
- ○ Large-group discussion. *(10 minutes)*

Record points from the discussion on the flipchart.

b) *What is your definition of 'values'?*

- ○ Personal reflection. *(5 minutes)*
- ○ Large or small group sharing and discussion. *(5 minutes)*

Facilitate and develop a definition on the flipchart. A dictionary definition should also be available.

c) *What are the three most important values for you today as an adult?*

- ○ Personal reflection. *(5 minutes)*
- ○ Large or small group sharing and discussion. *(5 minutes if large-group discussion, 10 minutes if small-group discussion)*

d) *What are the most important values in the organisation in which you work? When are those values compromised and why?*

- ○ Personal reflection. *(5 minutes)*
- ○ Large or small group sharing and discussion. *(10 minutes if small-group discussion, 20 minutes if large-group discussion)*

Pull together the discussion by comparing personal values with organisational values and ask the group:

- ○ Is there a mismatch? *If so,*
- ○ Why is there a mismatch?
- ○ What are the effects of this mismatch? *(10 minutes)*

1.4 Ask large group:

"What would you recommend people do to strengthen their values?"

Open discussion and end with summary. Ask group for conclusion. *(5 minutes)*

NOTE: Timing depends on group size. A confident facilitator is recommended.

Section 3

2. CREATIVE VALUES *(50 minutes)*

Purpose: To provide a creative outlet for authentic expression around lost values and to provide a forum for discussing and promoting right values.

Objective: For participants to develop an understanding of human values and an appreciation of how they have been diluted through time and history.

Method

2.1 Introduce the following task to be accomplished either as individuals or in groups of three:

If you were responsible for writing a message from Planet Earth to be sent in a spacecraft to other planets, what would you say about:

1) *Human values from a historical view?*

2) *What the human race values most today?*

3) *What you think the human race should value most?*

2.2 Allow 35–40 minutes to complete the task. If groups have been formed, time should allow each group to read its essay. If the task is done on an individual basis, then ask for volunteers to read their essays.

2.3 Focusing on one question at a time, ask for basic ideas and common ground and record responses on a flipchart.

3. ORGANISATIONAL VALUES *(30 minutes)*

Purpose: To give practical application to values discussion and to focus on specific behaviours and activities in the organisational setting.

Objective: For participants to become more aware of the role and importance of values in an organisational context.

Method

3.1 Divide large group into teams of three. Participants should work with different people.

3.2 Assign to each team one value from Section1of this book and provide copies of that particular Value Statement (or an extract from that Value Statement). There should be enough copies for everyone. Additionally, distribute a handout to each person containing the following questions:

1) *In your organisation, in what ways do you see the expression of this value in human behaviour/interactions?*

2) *In what situations is this value compromised or sacrificed and why?*

3) *How would you go about encouraging the growth and development of any of these values within your organisation?*

3.3 Ask each team member to read and reflect upon the above questions, then to discuss individual findings within the small group. *(15 minutes)*

3.4 Ask a group spokesperson for each team to report back briefly on the findings of, or insights gained, within the group.

4. INTEGRATING VALUES *(45 minutes)*

Purpose: To create a forum for 'defending' a value and, therefore, becoming closer to that and other values and to generate a lively and active discussion around the inter-relationship of values.

Objective: For participants to discuss and understand the linkage and inter-dependency between and among values.

Method

4.1 Divide the large group into teams of four. Again, effort should be made to mix people so they interact with different people.

4.2 Assign a different value to each team and distribute a copy of that particular Value Statement from this book to each member of the team. Use values other than those used previously.

4.3 Each team prepares the following argument: *(30 minutes)*

Why their particular value is the most important to the organisation and which three other values must be cultivated to support it?

4.4 Each team presents their argument. *(5 minutes each)*

Facilitate the large-group discussion to identify which value the whole group feels is really the most important and the three values that support it. Record comments on flipchart.

5. VALUES IN RELATIONSHIPS *(45 minutes)*

Purpose: To add a new dimension to a particular value and to facilitate discussion of that value in terms of behaviours, interactions and practical organisational examples.

Objective: For the participants to reflect upon and delve into one particular value as it relates to the self, others and the environment.

Method

5.1 Introduce a value which has not yet been discussed, e.g. respect.

5.2 Divide the large group into small groups 1, 2 and 3. Each small group focuses on one of the following:

Group 1: Respect for the self

Group 2: Respect for others

Group 3: Respect for the environment (organisation)

5.3 Give each group a handout of questions (one per person) and ask them to discuss and answer the following in light of the particular type of respect assigned to that group:

○ *What are the signs of self-respect?*

○ *What are the signs of the absence or lack of self-respect/respect?*

○ *What causes respect to develop in an individual/in a relationship/for the environment?*

○ *What stops respect from developing?*

○ *What are the methods to foster respect in this context?*

5.4 Each group presents its findings to the large group. *(5 minutes per group)*

5.5 Facilitate general discussion of the common findings.

5.6 *(Optional)* Provide each group with a copy of the Value Statement on respect from Section 1 of this book and ask group members to read, discuss and answer the following questions:

○ *How does this Value Statement add/alter our findings as a group?*

○ *Do we feel the statement is an accurate representation of the value of respect?*

5.7 Each group presents its findings in the light of the text. *(2 minutes per group)*

Section 3

6. RE-DEFINING VALUES *(15–25 minutes)*

Purpose: To provide a forum for further discussion and deeper understanding of values.

Objective: To revisit a particular value in the light of the *Living Our Values* text.

Method

6.1 Give each participant a copy of another Values Statement (or an extract from a Values Statement), which has not been discussed yet.

6.2 Provide a handout for each participant listing the following questions:

1. *What do you feel is the most important point or concept in this definition?*
2. *Why?*
3. *How would you recommend that concept or point be cultivated in human behaviour?*

6.3 Share and discuss as a large group.

6.4 *(Optional)* Divide large group into teams of three or four. Distribute to each group member the same handout of questions as above and provide a different Value Statement for each group. Discuss within the small group. If time allows, share insights within the large group.

7. LIVING OUR VALUES UPDATE *(45 minutes)*

Purpose: To provide an active training exercise to engage participants in a creative and intellectually stimulating process as a way of revisiting the Values Statements in this book.

Objective: To stimulate constructive thinking on values, and to provide an opportunity for participants to build on the ideas iin this book.

Method

7.1 Divide large group into teams of three of four.

7.2 Provide each team member with the text from one of the values in *Living Our Values*. Use a value not already discussed.

7.3 Ask each team to decide the following:

1. *What concepts don't we understand?*

2. *What is missing in this value statement?*

3. *What changes do we recommend?*

7.4 Each team reports back verbally.

COMMUNITIES

EXAMINING OUR CURRENT AND FUTURE VALUES WORKSHOP[1]

Introduction

This highly interactive workshop:

○ Invites participants to identify and define their own values

○ Creates a small-group dialogue in which participants reflect and gain insight into the practical application of values

○ Offers a group brainstorming and problem-solving session in which group members identify present and desired states of their communities and form community action teams to narrow the gap between the current and the ideal.

The workshop can be offered in its entirety or as separate modules.

Target Audience: Adult members of community groups, churches, temples and all other religious and spiritual organisations, clubs, professional associations and other civil society groups.

Duration: One day, or two half-days.

Methodology: Interactive lecture, large and small-group discussion, silent introspection, guided visualisation, individual and/or group brainstorming and action planning.

Subject Matter: Intrinsic Values, Common Values, Living the Values, Community Action Planning.

Materials: Easels, flipchart paper, masking tape, markers, lined writing paper, large index cards, pencils, CD player and light instrumental music (optional).

---

1 Designed by Ken O'Donnell.

1: INTRINSIC VALUES ICEBREAKER

(5 minutes)

Purpose: To become aware that every single object has some intrinsic value, which is related to its function. The leader can then bridge the topic to human beings, leading to the conclusion that our values have a lot to do with our function. Keep discussion light and try to get participants to draw that conclusion.

Objective: For participants to introduce themselves to each other in a fun way.

1.1 Seat participants in a semicircle, or circle, and ask them to select an object in the room with which they can identify. Ask them to introduce themselves, one by one, as that object and to add a 'because' statement that identifies the object's intrinsic value. For example:

"I am the window because others can see through me to the world."

"I am the chair because I am stable."

"I am the light because I illuminate."

"I am the air because I am light. Even though others can't see me, I am important."

NOTE: If group members seem to feel self-conscious about using the "I am" phrase, they can say, "I identify with such-and-such an object because…".

2: SHARING AND UNDERSTANDING VALUES

(30 minutes)

Purpose: To bring people closer together through sharing and understanding common values.

When participants see the similarity of values from the stories they 'hold dear,' that will set a common ground for further work on other values. In the community context, it is possible that many different ethnic backgrounds will be present in the group. As such, participants will discover the commonality between them regardless of cultural backgrounds (especially if they have remembered myths and fables of their respective countries). The leader should guide the group to the realisation of these common denominators.

Objective: For participants to feel a sense of closeness and to become aware of the commonality of values through the cross-fertilisation of experiences.

2.1 Help participants relax and become aware of the 'here and now' by asking them to follow the thoughts below. Participants may close their eyes if they want to. Play ambient music (*optional*).

Listen for all the sounds you can possibly hear – traffic, voices, movement, birds and so on. Feel the movement of the air and feel the temperature. Become aware of your own breathing. Just be the observer of all these things and situate yourself in the centre of the space around you. In the same way that you are surrounded by all these things, you are at the centre of all your present situations – roles, responsibilities, relationships, routines – so bring yourself to the centre of these and, again, just observe them as a spectator.

In this state of calm observation, try to remember the most important story you have heard in your life – a story that has somehow had a deep impact on you. The story can be a myth, a fable, a movie, or even a real story. Go through the details of the story in your mind and think about its meaning.

When the story is clear, ask yourself, "What aspect of my inner world has this story evoked?" *Is it love, happiness, realisation, goodness? What comes to your mind? Now just leave the story aside and stay with the feeling that it has brought up.*

Open your eyes, but allow them to rest and try to stay with the feeling for a few more moments.

2.2 Ask participants to divide into pairs. Announce that it is better when the two members of the pair do not know each other at all, or at least not very well. Instruct that first one, then the other, should share his or her story and the message that caused some impact. Each person should take three minutes to share his or her story, followed by a five-minute discussion between the two on the values contained in both stories.

2.3 Bring them back to the large-group setting and ask for comments about the learning points of the experience and the following discussion.

NOTE: Invite participants to share insights or lessons learned only, not to repeat the whole story to the large group.

2.4 As participants share, record the essence of their comments on a flipchart or white board. This can be done by dividing the space into two columns, as follows:

COMMENTS	CORE VALUE CONTAINED IN COMMENT
1.	1.
2.	2.
3.	3.
4.	4.

Section 3

3: VALUES DIALOGUE *(45–60 minutes)*

Purpose: The aim of the dialogue process is to set off, or spark, a human flow of energy so that authentic sharing can take place, which allows each participant to gain true insights and realisations.

Objectives: For participants to focus on the self and another person who has been significant in their lives while exploring the impact of behaviour as it relates to values.

To share insights and, in that process, to feel a real sense of closeness and community.

3.1 Introduce the 'Ground Rules' of the meeting. See examples of Ground Rules on p. 70.

3.2 Divide participants into random groups of 5 or 6. Allow about 15 minutes for the group to do the following:

Ask them to relax and go into silence by becoming an observer of the things around them (as in Step 2.1 above).

Ask them to write down the name of the person in their life they feel closest to. Divide the page into two columns:

BEHAVIOUR	VALUE DEMONSTRATED BY BEHAVIOUR
1.	1.
2.	2.
3.	3.

Ask them to think about the behaviour that characterises the relationship, then:

a) write down three aspects in the left-hand column describing why they consider that behaviour important, and

b) in the right-hand column, write beside each of the three aspects the value that is demonstrated by the behaviour.

Prioritise the three values and underline the main one.

3.3 Announce that participants should share the value they have underlined with the other members of the small group. Types of questions to be addressed in this sharing follow:

○ *What does (the name of the value underlined) mean to you?*

○ *How is (the value) important in relationships?*

○ *How is (the value) important in the context of the work we do in our (community) group?*

○ *What are the systems and structures necessary to support these values?*

○ *What sort of behaviour does that lead to?*

○ *How can we use that behaviour (that value) to strengthen our work?*

3.4 *(Optional)* In a large-group discussion, you may want to ask participants to share learning experiences or insights gained (not necessarily points discussed).

Section 3

4: LARGE-GROUP BRAINSTORM AND COMMUNITY ACTION TEAMS *(2–3 hours)*

Purpose: For participants to focus quickly on what needs to be done and to plan immediate action steps.

Objective: For participants to focus on six exercises, which examine present values, and to set up an ongoing process to strengthen and confirm what has come out of the workshop.

Exercises 1 to 4 are addressed within the large group and the leader records all ideas on separate flipcharts for each theme. (It is best to post each flipchart sheet as it is completed, so participants can refer to ideas already generated. Most groups would not have more than one flipchart sheet.)

Exercises 5 and 6 are discussed within smaller community action teams of five or six members. If the overall group is comprised of people who are meeting only once, then the action plan and values discussed in Exercises 5 and 6 need to be created and implemented only at the individual level.

Before each exercise, ask the participants to reflect in silence before suggesting their ideas.

Exercise 1 – Present State

Question: *What are our main current strengths as a group in terms of ideals and behaviours?* (Record all ideas)

Exercise 2 – Where Do We Want to Go from Here?

Question: *How do we see our future six months from now if everything we want to do actually happens?* (Record all ideas)

Exercise 3 – Possible Obstacles

Question: *Knowing ourselves and knowing where we want to go, what sort of obstacles or barriers could come up in our work and relationships which could prevent us from getting where we want to go?* (Record all ideas)

Exercise 4 – Aims

Question: *Taking into account our present state, future destination and possible obstacles, what are the three main aims that we have to work on right now?* (Record all ideas and then have group members vote on each idea. The three aims receiving most votes will be issues to address in Exercises 5 and 6.)

Exercise 5 – Setting Up Community Action Teams

To form groups, invite participants to self-select the aim in which they are most interested.

Ask the group to elect someone to act as facilitator to record the group's ideas.

Question: *What can we plan for the next month in real terms?*

Determine who, how, when, what and where in sufficient detail to be realistic. In other words, record each specific action for accomplishing a task, list who is responsible and set a deadline for carrying it out. At the next meeting, these 'next steps' would be revisited.

Exercise 6 – Setting Up the Values

Question: *Considering the results of all the other themes, what are the three main values we need to practise and implement to bring success to our plans?*

Optional Methodology (for Exercises 1 to 4)

Recommended if the entire group consists of more than 18–20 participants.

1. Participants remain seated with those with whom they dialogued in previous exercise.

2. Hand out large index cards to each group.

3. Ask participants to reflect silently on the theme in question (you may want to use the first part of Step 2 to relax everyone).

4. Ask participants to write down the first three ideas that come to mind for that theme.

5. Ask participants to prioritise the ideas, underlining the most interesting or important one.

6. Instruct participants to share the idea underlined among members of the small group.

7. Carry out this process through Exercise 3.

Section 3

8. For Exercise 4, the small group reaches consensus on the three best ideas for the main aim.

9. Each group records on three separate index cards the three best ideas for the main aim.

10. Each group hands its index cards to the leader, who arranges them in categories and posts them on the wall.

11. The whole group of participants chooses the three best ideas for main aim.

12. Move to Exercise 5.

COMMUNITIES

CARING FOR THE ENVIRONMENT WORKSHOP[1]

Duration: 2 hours and 30 minutes.

Purpose: To encourage participants to appreciate the Earth, connect with its current poor condition and be inspired to help it.

Exercise 1: Appreciating the Earth *(35 minutes)*

1. Welcome and introduction. *(5 minutes)*

2. Ask the participants to close their eyes for a few minutes, relax and visualise a peaceful scene in nature conducive to calm and well-being, for example on the top of a mountain, or by a riverside, or the seashore.

3. Ask them to look at our planet from space and enjoy its beauty. For an English-speaking audience you can play the song 'From A Distance'. *(5 minutes)*

4. Ask them to write down 3 of the main qualities of the Earth with 1 or 2 examples to illustrate their ideas. *(5 minutes)*

5. Ask them to share their vision with their neighbour. *(10 minutes)*

6. Share the different qualities in the plenary. Appoint someone to write down the different qualities on a flipchart. *(10 minutes)*

Exercise 2: Developing Compassion for the Earth *(45 minutes)*

Play some ambient music and take the participants back to the experience of visualising our planet and tell them that if the Earth could talk, she probably would have quite a bit to communicate to human beings. *(5 minutes)*

---

1 Designed by Valeriane Bernard and taken from the Brahma Kumaris Environmental web page http://environment.brahmakumaris.org

Ask the participants to imagine that the Earth is writing a letter to human beings, and:

○ Try to 'feel' the message and the wisdom that the Earth wants to share with us and write it down. *(10 minutes)*

○ Read their letter in groups of 3. *(15 minutes)*

○ Share the essence of what they have experienced with the whole group. *(15 minutes)*

Exercise 3: Changing Our Behaviour *(70 minutes)*

Now that participants have 'linked' with the wisdom of the planet, ask them to question their own attitudes towards the environment. In a peaceful atmosphere, with music, ask them to:

○ Visualise their behaviour, attitude and efforts to help and protect the environment in their everyday life .*(5 minutes)*

Identify and write down 3 habits they have which contribute to the protection of the environment. *(10 minutes)*

○ Write down 3 habits they have which are not environmentally friendly but could be improved quite easily .*(10 minutes)*

Organise the participants into groups of 4. Ask them to:

○ Share the three habits that they will improve;

○ Create a charter for the protection of the environment, which each member of the group will commit himself/herself to put in practice in daily life; *(20 minutes)*

○ Read out their own charter in the plenary session; *(15 minutes)*

○ Appoint one volunteer per group to email (or post) a copy of the group's charter to all the group members within 3-4 days so as to remind them of the behaviours they have committed themselves to change. *(5 minutes)*

Conclusions *(10 minutes)*

○ Ask participants what they have learned.

○ Speak a commentary (with ambient music) on the theme of healing Mother Earth, including some of the insights and action plans of the participants.

COMMUNITIES

FULFILLING THE GLOBAL VISION WORKSHOP

Introduction

Your vision for yourself and the world will stand on the foundation of your values. The direction you take in life is a result of the values you choose. At every step you are making value judgements according to the priority you have placed on certain values.

Identifying values is empowering. It clarifies what you stand for. It gives you commitment to following those highest values and gives you the basis on which to choose the right course of action at the right time.

Sharing values is uplifting. As people in groups, organizations, societies and in the world share values, they realize that the core values which bind us together are so much greater than the things that set us apart.

Aims

(a) to identify the core values which underlie The Global Vision Statement;

(b) to identify the barriers which prevent us from adopting and living those core values;

(c) to develop strategic action plans (organizational, community or personal) in order to overcome those barriers and thus make The Global Vision Statement a reality.

Exercise 1: Introduction *(20 minutes)*

○ Welcome

○ Give the background of the Global Cooperation project;

○ Present The Global Vision Statement;

❍ Identify the core values underlying the Statement;

❍ Divide participants into twelve small groups, one for each part of the Statement.

Exercise 2: Values Workshop *(90–120 minutes)*

Each small group:

❍ Explores what values are from a personal perspective;

❍ Discusses what values underlie their allocated part of the Statement and can enable it to become a reality;

❍ Agree on the three main underlying values of all the parts of the Statement.

Small groups feedback to the whole group which then discusses and agrees on the three core values that underlie the whole Global Vision Statement.

Exercise 3: Barriers to Success *(90–120 minutes)*

Divide participants into four small groups to:

❍ Identify barriers in bringing the above agreed values into action at personal, organizational and community levels;

❍ Agree on the three key obstacles;

❍ Identify the problems, contradictions or value-clashes that cause obstacles to arise or lead to paralysis in the implementation of plans.

Each group presents to whole group which agrees on three major barriers.

Exercise 4: Strategies for Success *(90–120 minutes)*

Divide participants back into the same four groups to:

❍ Discuss and develop strategic action plans that will help overcome the identified barriers and allow the chosen values to be expressed more fully in personal, organizational and community life;

❍ Agree on the six strongest plans.

Each group presents its six agreed strategic action plans to the whole group, which reviews and reflects on all the core values, barriers and plans.

Conclusion *(30 minutes)*

- ○ Evaluate the day's proceedings;
- ○ Ask everyone to make a personal commitment to carry out their chosen strategic action plans;
- ○ Make closing remarks.

FAMILIES

BUILDING FAMILY RELATIONSHIPS WORKSHOPS[1]

Introduction

These workshops are designed to enable families to do things together in a learning atmosphere of positivity and lightness. They combine fun, creativity, silent reflection and group interaction to encourage positive expression. Quality of life is first experienced in the home and that is dependent on the quality of the family relationships. These worksops help families do things together by

○ creating a shared vision;

○ celebrating togetherness;

○ experiencing mutual respect;

○ sharing values and mutual responsibility.

Activities throughout the workshops will touch each participant, tapping inner beauty and unleashing spiritual power, thus bringing back vibrancy, happiness and quality to their lives.

Target Audience: Ideally 20–25 participants per workshop session (about 3–5 families). All family members, with the exception of very young children, should be present at the same workshop.

Duration: Workshops 1–3 can be run as three consecutive sessions lasting between two hours and two and a half hours each. The workshops also can be used independently.

Workshop 4 is designed to be run as three consecutive inter-connected parts.

Methodology: Talk, small-group discussion, group creative activity, large-group presentation, creative visualisation.

Experiential learning methodology includes three main steps:

---

1 Created by Rebecca Ortega, a human resource development consultant based in the Philippines.

1) Doing and sharing together through structured learning activities;

2) Learning together through collecting and analysing data from experiences and drawing conclusions from those experiences;

3) Planning/acting together to encourage application of learning.

Materials: See individual exercises.

Remember

1. Family is not just a word, it is a VALUE.

2. Self-respect is a core value in a healthy functioning family.

3. Healthy communication is a necessity for healthy family relationships.

4. Harmony is the heart of a happy family.

Section 3

1. APPRECIATING THE STRENGTHS OF OUR FAMILY

Family is not just a word – it is a VALUE

Objectives:

❍ To identify and clarify shared family experiences;

❍ To agree on and appreciate shared values of the family;

❍ To feel proud of our family values and to take actions to share those values with others.

Duration: 2 hours and 30 minutes.

Materials: Easel, flipchart paper, masking tape, markers, boxes of crayons (one per family), lined writing paper, pencils.

1 Doing/Sharing Together

1.1 Begin with a moment of silence. Ask participants to "Keep a good wish in your mind for your family." Begin with "May we…". After the silence, ask three participants to share their wishes.

1.2 Explain the significance of a flag, brand image or advert carrying the symbols of a person's or clan's significant achievements, vision and mission, distinguishing characteristics and significant contribution to society.

1.3 Explain the *purpose* of the activity: to create your own family flag or image based on the following questions:

❍ What is your family's greatest achievement?

❍ What are your family's happiest shared moments?

❍ What would your family consider as your biggest resource or wealth?

❍ What would your family consider as your contribution to society and the world?

❍ What are three qualities, which best describe your family?

Answers to the above questions should be in words.

1.4 Explain the steps of the activity:

❍ Discuss and agree upon your answers to these questions. Decide on what symbols you will use to draw your answers. *(15–20 minutes)*

○ Use flipchart paper, crayons, pencil and markers to draw your coat of arms/brand image/advert (about 12" x 8") on the centre of the flipchart paper (10–15 minutes)

○ When your flag/brand image/advert is finished, decide upon and rehearse how you will present your work (15 minutes). Be creative! You may decide to sing, dance, or do a sketch.

NOTE: Families should be instructed that each presentation should be *no more than 5–7 minutes.*

1.5 Large-group (all families) presentations. Each family presents its work while the rest listen and take note of the uniqueness of each presentation. The audience should affirm each presentation.

2 Learning Together

2.1 After the presentations, each family regroups and members answer the following questions:

○ How did you feel throughout the activity?

○ What did the activity do for our family? How did it happen that way?

○ What values do we have as a family?

○ Of the many values we shared, which three do we think and feel matter the most to us?

A 'family reporter' should be elected to report back during the large-group reporting of the learning and insights.

2.2 Large-group reporting. Each family reporter shares with the whole group the collective learning of his/her family.

2.3 Integration/Talk. Share your observations. Some suggestions follow:

> ***On the process:*** Emphasise the beauty and importance of doing things together in an atmosphere of positivity, unconditional love, lightness and fun. Positive interaction enhances relationships.

> ***On the content:*** Build on the values, which surfaced during the reporting. Help participants draw the conclusion that family is more than just a word – it is a VALUE.

Section 3

3. Acting Together

3.1 Regroup as families and sit in circles. Rewrite three shared values in a credo form, approximately 5–10 lines only. Before beginning, the leader should explain that a credo is a set of fundamental beliefs, or guiding principles. Each family might start with:

We, the _____ family,

believe in and value _____

_____,

and _____.

We are_____etc

3.2 Large-group sharing. Each family takes a turn reciting its respective credo.

2. LOVING MYSELF AND OTHERS

Self-Respect is a Core Value in a Healthy Functioning Family

Objective: To identify special qualities of each family member in terms of:

    a) What each one knows about the self;

    b) What others recognise and acknowledge; and

    c) What each one feels are his/her specialties and potential.

Duration: 2 hours 30 minutes.

Materials: Easels, flipchart paper, masking tape, markers, bond paper, pencils, crayons, old colourful magazines, scissors, paste/glue, Value Statement on respect from Section 1 of this book.

1 Doing/Sharing Together

1.1 Visualisation

(Read slowly and softly) *In silence, visualize yourself settled in your favourite spot – anywhere in the world… You are enjoying the surroundings. Suddenly, you see yourself appear in the distance and you begin walking towards you, the person who is settled in that favourite spot. The person walking towards you – this other you – walks happily and with confidence. The face looks so peaceful and content. You look so beautiful and radiant. You observe and appreciate yourself … What special qualities do you see?… What special talents or skills? … What else do you think you can be, or do, if given the opportunity? … Enjoy looking at yourself … Feel your uniqueness. You are special and valuable… Now… slowly… bring your awareness to this room, which is full of special people, including yourself and your very own special family.*

1.2 Create a self-poster *(20–25 minutes)*

Browse through the available magazines and select three pictures/symbols, which describe how you visualised yourself. As you do this, keep the feelings you experienced during the visualisation exercise. Cut the pictures/symbols and paste them on the centre of the bond paper. This becomes your self-poster.

1.3 Write on the self-poster the meaning of the symbolic collage in terms of:

    a) *What you know about yourself (on the top of the sheet).*

Section 3

b) *What others recognise in you (on the right side).*

c) *What you feel are your specialties and your potential (on the left side).*

After the self-posters are finished, set them aside and group as a family.

1.4 Small-group sharing *(30 minutes)*

As a family, sit in a circle.

Each member takes turns as the receiver of loveful affirmations. The others become the bestowers, who shower the receiver with recognition of all the special qualities they see.

After the affirmations, the receiver responds by expressing gratitude, then by sharing his/her self-poster. The receiver identifies three qualities, which he/she strongly wants to continue developing.

The bestowers affirm and give blessings for success.

(*Optional:* To empower the receiver's effort, bestowers can give their blessings in chorus. For example, "*Becky, you are a determined soul. Becky, you are a beautiful soul. Becky, you are a happy soul.*" While listening, the receiver takes in and keeps the awareness of those blessings in his/her mind and heart.)

2 Learning Together

2.1 Individually, take 10–15 minutes to answer the following questions

- *Which part did you enjoy most? Which did you enjoy least?*
- *What did you discover about yourself based on what you heard about yourself?*
- *How do you feel about yourself at this moment? How do you feel about each member of your family?*
- *How will you maintain your state of self-respect?*
- *What support do you need from your family in this effort?*

2.2 Small-group sharing *(20–25 minutes)*

Regroup as a family and sit in a circle. Share your reflections and learning. Assign a family reporter to take notes of what (content) and how (process) the family shared.

2.3 Large-group reporting *(20–25 minutes)*

Each reporter presents the summary of his/her family's sharing session from both content and process standpoints.

2.4 Integration/Talk *(5–10 minutes)*

Summarise learning and practical application points.

Other thoughts for the talk:

○ Self-respect (also known as self-worth or self-esteem) and mutual respect are essential factors in developing and maintaining a healthy functioning family.

○ Healthy relationships imply the giving and taking of positive qualities: peace, love, cooperation and so on. Giving and taking improve harmony in relationships. To do that effectively, we need self-respect.

○ If we are aware of our own value, we are strong and have self-confidence. It is then easy to recognise the qualities of others. If we lack self-respect, we may feel incompleteness within and may tend to see weaknesses in others as a reflection of the void within ourselves. With self-respect, we are less likely to foster conditional relationships to fill the 'gap' and more likely to share without expecting any return.

3 Planning /Acting Together

3.1 Small-group work *(20–25 minutes)*

Families regroup and sit in a circle. In light of the large-group learnings and the talk, create a list of 10 'Do's to practise the value of respect and enhance each other's self-respect.

3.2 Print on a flipchart your family 'Do's which should become family norms. Each family member signs it at the bottom. Families are encouraged to post the chart when they return home.

3.3 Families are instructed to take 20 minutes at the end of each week to check to what extent the family has followed 'our family norms'. Members who have practised or have followed the norms should be affirmed.

3.4 Close the session with a few moments of reflection. Remain for a few seconds in silence before ending the workshop.

Section 3

3. IMPROVING FAMILY COMMUNICATION

Healthy Communication is a Necessity for Healthy Family Relationships

Objectives:

❍ To experience how positive interaction can build understanding and friendship.

❍ To identify key values in listening and speaking to enhance positive communication.

❍ To identify two values for practice by each family.

Duration: 2 hours.

Materials: Easel, flipchart paper, masking tape, markers.

1 Doing/Sharing Together

1.1 Begin with silent reflection. Ask participants to recall one positive, memorable experience they had (recent or distant past) in the family. Identify the overwhelming quality of that experience. Was it courage, happiness, success, love, tenderness, or another quality? Stay in that experience and enjoy or relive that quality again.

1.2 'Round-Robin' sharing. Group into threes (random, preferably not with a member of the participant's family). Participants can 'count off' A, B, C, or leader can assign who will be A, B and C. Follow the role chart below during sharing session.

Participants	A	B	C
Round 1	Speaker	Listener	Observer
Round 2	Observer	Speaker	Listener
Round 3	Listener	Observer	Speaker

Roles:

Speaker shares for 3 minutes his/her story.

Listener repeats the story using the first person. Take no longer than 3 minutes.

Observer watches the interaction and keeps the time.

1.3 After all have shared stories, call everyone back to the large group.

2 Learning Together

2.1 Ask the following questions:

- ❍ *How did you feel listening to your story being retold?*
- ❍ *What quality was apparent in the story you listened to?*
- ❍ *How do you feel about each other now?*

2.2 Draw out the qualities of positive communication by asking participants to identify qualities they observed when:

	SPEAKING	LISTENING
1.		
2.		
3.		
4.		

2.3 Integration/Talk. Share your observations. Some suggestions follow.

- ❍ Communication and understanding are possible when we share our qualities in a positive way.
- ❍ It only takes a few minutes to 'make or keep a friend' when we communicate positively.
- ❍ Listening is not just hearing the words spoken but also acknowledging the feelings behind those words and, most importantly, recognising the qualities of the other person.
- ❍ Positive communication builds bridges and establishes interconnectedness.

3 Planning/Acting Together

3.1 Families regroup and sit in a circle. Spend 15 minutes identifying the main qualities, or values family members need to practise to enhance positive communication. Each family should decide upon two specific values that members need to practise most.

3.2 Show a simple matrix of behaviours to practise a value.

Example: Value of Tolerance – what should we . . .

STOP DOING	START DOING	CONTINUE DOING
Blaming each other	Helping each other correct mistakes	Affirming each other's good behaviour or actions

NOTE: The three columns do not have to match. Limit: One behaviour per column. Make behaviours very specific.

3.3 End session with a few moments of silence. Reflect on the values the families have adopted.

4. CO-CREATING HARMONY IN THE FAMILY

Harmony is the heart of a happy family

Brief Description:

This workshop is designed for three consecutive weeks/sessions with, or without, an external facilitator or moderator. Choose a time each week (preferably Saturday or Sunday) when the entire family can sit together for a structured conversation. Ideally, all family members (including extended family members who are living in the same house) should be present to actively participate.

The workshop design makes use of the *Jewels for Life* virtue cards published by the Brahma Kumaris Raja Yoga Centre, Iceland (lotushus@lotushus.is).

A copy of the cards can be found at the end of this workshop. You may print these cards on coloured paper, or create your own.

Objectives of the Family Workshops:

By the end of the third session, the family and family members will have experienced a renewed sense of harmony by:

- ○ Deepening their sense of self respect and appreciating the positive qualities of each family member
- ○ Appreciating the process of giving and taking of non-threatening, positive feedback among family members
- ○ Creating an easy, light and playful atmosphere conducive for meaningful and loving interaction in the family.

Materials Needed and Pre-Workshop Preparation:

- ○ A room (big enough for 15 participants) where everyone can sit in a circle around a low table
- ○ 2 or 3 decks of virtue cards
- ○ *Soul Refresh* forms (one for each family member). A copy of the *Soul Refresh* form is found on page 127.

Duration of Session: 2–2½ hours per workshop session.

Number of Participants: 10–15. If a family is only 5 (or less) invite more families to join to make up the numbers. Choose families who are close friends.

Part 1: APPRECIATING OURSELVES

Materials Needed:

1. CD player and a selection of fast music
2. Three or four soft cushions or pillows
3. Copies of the STAR sheet
4. Ask each participant to bring his or her photo (2" x 2") for the session
5. Glue stick or paste bottle

1.1 Doing and Being Together *(60 minutes)*

1.1.1 Opening remarks. Convene the family members around a low table. Re-assure the family that the activities during the three workshop sessions (over three consecutive weeks) will be fun and creative.

1.1.2 Self Introduction *(15–30 minutes)*

○ Start the activity by asking the question *"Why do I love me, Becky (if that's the leader's name)?* Hugging the pillow or cushion she completes the statement: *"I love you, Becky because you are always happy and smiling."*

○ Pass the pillow to the person on your right.

○ Play fast music. When the music stops, the one with the pillow will complete the statement *"I love you, _____, because you are _____."*

○ After that, the music plays again and the process repeats until all participants have said something about themselves.

1.1.3 Affirmation *(15–30 minutes)*

○ Take the pillow from the last person who finished then say, *"Yes Jimmy (if that's the name of the last person who was holding the pillow), I love you because you are jolly and friendly."*

○ Jimmy passes the pillow to the person on his right and says, *"I love you, (name of the person) because _____."*

○ Everyone takes turns to affirm and appreciate the person on their right side.

○ When the pillow reaches the last one in the circle, they appreciate or affirm the person on their left.

1.1.4 Sharing Our Feelings and Expectations *(30 minutes)*

a) *Ask the following questions:*

- ○ Was it difficult or easy to say "l love me because ____." Why?
- ○ How did you feel listening to someone who says that s/he loves you? Why?
- ○ How could we be more comfortable when receiving an affirmation from others?
- ○ How could we develop a daily habit of affirming the self by realising our virtues and positive qualities?

b) *Explain the workshop series:*

- ○ We get to know ourselves by others affirming our good and positive qualities. And by listening to the good and positive qualities of others we get to appreciate them more.
- ○ What do you think will happen when we get to know ourselves better?
- ○ What good things will happen when we get to know others better (both our own family members and family friends)?
- ○ We are going to be together for three consecutive weeks to deepen our appreciation of ourselves as well as our family members. Could each of us create a wish for our own family and ourselves? Example: "After three weeks, I wish to have more love for myself and my family members." Or, "I wish that my brothers and sisters will not tease or make fun of me any more."
- ○ Ask everyone to share a wish for the self and her/his family.

1.2 Appreciating and Being Together *(60 minutes)*

1.2.1 Ask the participants to sit with their own family in a smaller circle. Distribute enough STAR sheets for each member of the family and a pillow. Give the following instructions:

Start with the youngest member of your family. Take a STAR sheet and paste her/his photo on it. Let the STAR (family member being focused on) sit facing everyone. Other family members take turns to give the good qualities they observe or experience from the STAR. Tell a story to exemplify the qualities of the STAR.

Fill in the STAR sheet with the qualities each one appreciates about her/him. Write the qualities around the points of the STAR as in the example below.

Ask participants to take home the STAR sheets and post them on a board to remind everyone about the family's 'mine' of positive qualities daily.

1.3 Close Family Workshop

Play soft, gentle music. Invite participants for silent reflection:

As we sit here after experiencing these wonderful activities, we begin to realise how lucky and fortune we are to belong to our family. (Pause) *We all have beautiful inner qualities. We are innately positive and good.* (Pause) *As we practise and live these qualities they become our gifts to each other and the world.* (Pause) *Let our thoughts and feelings be filled with goodness.*

Part 2: LIVING OUR QUALITIES

Materials Needed:

1. CD player and a CD audio selection of meditative music
2. Copies of SOUL REFRESH sheet for all the participants plus a few extra just in case
3. Virtue cards

Duration of Session: 2 hours

2.1 Doing and Being Together *(60 minutes)*

2.1.1 Opening Remarks

Welcome the participating families and their respective members for the second session of *Co-Creating Harmony in the Family.*

2.1.2 Review of Last Week

a) Play soft music and invite them for a few moments of silence to reflect on the gains of last week's activities in their respective families:

As I sit here, I look back over the past week. What positive changes have there been in myself and my family since last week's workshop? (Pause) *How did I use my qualities when I related and interacted with my family members?* (Pause) *Let me visualise my family – full of love and enjoying a peaceful atmosphere and harmonious relationships.* (Pause) *I love myself and I love my family. I am happy and glad that I am a member of this wonderful family.*

b) Invite everyone to share some positive stories about the effects of last week's activities on appreciation and affirmation.

2.1.3 Introduce *Soul Refresh*

Explain that the idea is to use three key virtues to manage our life for a week. Virtues make our lives and relationships sweet, fragrant and joyful. When we live our positive qualities, or virtues, our lives become obstacle-free; problems and excuses are transformed into solutions. Let us experiment on using virtues in our practical life.

2.2 *Soul Refresh* Activity

2.2.1 Introduction

- ○ Ask participants to go into their own family group.
- ○ Give a deck of virtue cards to each family.

Section 3

○ Distribute also *Soul Refresh* forms to all the participants.

○ Ask them to write their names and date on the forms.

○ Ask one family member of each group to be in charge of shuffling the cards and spreading them (face down) on the table.

○ Explain that the purpose of the activity is to choose three cards, which will guide their choices, decisions, relationships and interactions for seven days. Why seven days? Seven days is enough time to create a good habit to transform your life.

2.2.2 *Soul Refresh* Procedure

a) The first virtue card is your BLESSING card.

○ Think about the next seven days and ask yourself: *"What virtue or positive quality do I need to practise during the coming week to bring easy success and lightness in my life while relating to people and dealing with different situations?"*

○ Pick any card from the deck of cards.

○ Reflect on that virtue while you wait for everyone else to choose their card.

○ After everyone has picked his or her virtue, each in turn reads aloud the definition of their virtue.

○ Share your insight about your blessing card.

○ Write down on your *Soul Refresh* form the virtue definition.

○ Return all the cards and shuffle again.

b) The second virtue card is your SUPPORT card.

○ Knowing your blessing card, think: *"What virtue will provide the balance to ensure easy victory in all my undertakings or endeavours during the week?"*

○ Pick a card.

○ Reflect on the virtue while you wait for everyone to get his or her card.

○ After everyone has picked his or her virtue, take turns to read aloud your virtue definition.

○ Write down on your *Soul Refresh* form the virtue definition of your second card.

○ Return your card to the rest of the deck and shuffle again.

c) The third virtue card is your CHALLENGE card.

○ Ask yourself: *"What virtue should I practise to face possible difficulty, confusion and uncertainty that could come in front of me during the coming week?"*

○ Again pick a card.

○ Reflect on the virtue definition while you wait for everyone to get their card.

○ After everyone has picked his or her virtue, take turns to read aloud your virtue definition.

○ Write down on your *Soul Refresh* form/sheet the virtue definition of your third card.

○ Return your card to the rest of the deck.

2.3 Sharing Insights and Feelings

2.3.1 After the *Soul Refresh* activity encourage the participants to share their feelings and insights. Ask

○ How do you feel about the three cards you have picked?

○ What message or meaning did you get from your blessing and support cards?

○ What is the message you are getting from your challenge card?

○ What did you learn about yourself from this activity?

2.3.2 Ask about their family members:

○ Listening to their chosen virtue cards what insight or learning did you have about one or some of your family members?

○ How do you feel about your family right now?

Keeping a Chart of Our Three Virtues for the Week

A chart is a way of monitoring how well we are doing. It gives us an accurate picture of the changes we are making in our life.

○ Throughout the day, practise or apply the virtues.

○ Check how they are helping you to remain light and happy.

○ At night before you go to bed, note down the wonders you have experienced throughout the day and any mistakes you have made and visualise how you could correct them tomorrow.

○ Let go of any disappointment or worry.

○ Sleep comfortably and peacefully after checking your chart of success.

2.4 Closing the Workshop

Invite the participants to relax and enjoy the following commentary/ meditation:

As we sit here, we realise that virtues are naturally part of every soul. Goodness is every soul's natural desire. (Pause)

I want peace because I am a being of peace.

I need love because I am a being of love. (Pause)

Purity, peace, joy, love, truth, mercy and spiritual power are the beauty of the soul. (Pause)

I visualise myself as a being of light and might! (Pause)…

Part 3: MOVING TOGETHER TO THE FUTURE

Materials needed:

1. CD player and a selection of meditative music

2. Make copies of the *Soul Refresh* forms

3. Virtue cards

4. Art materials: large easel paper, boxes of crayons, coloured pencils and marking pens, a roll of masking tape, assorted coloured papers, old magazines for cut-outs, etc.

5. Request each participating family to bring one food dish, enough for all the participants to share after the workshop

Duration of session: 2 hours

3.1 Doing and Being Together *(75 minutes)*

3.1.1 Opening Remarks

Welcome the participants to the third and last session of *Co-Creating Harmony in the Family.*

3.1.2 Creating a Vision for Our Family

Play meditative music and invite participants to reflect in silence:

As we sit here in silence, let us visualise a model family where there is love, respect, harmony, cooperation and a sense of belonging. (Pause)

What do I see and touch in the home of this model family? (Pause)

How do family members interact and relate to each other? (Pause)

Visualise your family as the model family. How would it feel being part of such a model family? (Pause)

Listen to your conversation. What words and feelings are being exchanged among the members? (Pause)

Visualise a typical weekend in your model family.

3.1.3 Share Qualities

Ask the participants to sit together with their own family and share the qualities they visualised in the exercise.

3.1.4 Create a Vision

Come up with a consensus vision of a model family after all members have shared their experience.

Section 3

3.1.5 Prepare a Presentation

Plan and produce a creative presentation of your model family through sketch, song and dance, or a visual portrait of a model family. Provide the art materials to the participants.

3.1.6 Vision Presentation of Participating Families

Invite the families to gather together to watch the different vision presentations. As they watch the creative presentations, identify similar as well as unique aspects of the different family presentations.

3.1.7 Identify Common and unique Aspects of the Visions

Assist the entire group to identify:

- ○ Common and unique aspects of the family visions;
- ○ Values common to all the families and the values unique to each family.

3.2 Making Our Vision a Reality *(15 minutes)*

Ask the participants to go back to their family groups.

Guide the families to accomplish the next activity:

3.2.1 Virtues of Family Harmony

Each family is given a deck of virtue cards. As a family they choose the virtues for the week, which they as a family could practise to make their vision a reality. Cards are shuffled and laid face down on the table.

BLESSING cards

- ○ Everyone silently asks *"Which two virtues or positive qualities do we need to practise together this week to create easy success and lightness in our family life and relationships?"*
- ○ The whole family stops for a moment of silence as they internalise the question above.
- ○ In silence, two members pick a blessing card each.
- ○ Each card is read aloud for everyone to hear.
- ○ Every member shares her/his reflection or insight about the two blessing cards for the family.
- ○ All the family write down the blessing card definitions on their *Soul Refresh* form.
- ○ The deck of cards is shuffled again and laid face down on the table.

SUPPORT VIRTUE card

- Everyone picks a virtue, which will support the family blessing cards asking themselves: *"What virtue do I need to practise this week to provide the balance to ensure lightness and harmony in our interactions and family life?"*

- Reflect on the virtue which you picked as you wait for everyone to get their cards.

- After everyone has picked their virtue, they take turns to read aloud their virtue definition.

- Write down on your *Soul Refresh* form the virtue definition of your second card.

- Return the cards to the deck and shuffle again.

CHALLENGE card

- Ask a family member to pick a card, which addresses the question *"What virtue should we all practise to minimize clashes of personalities and disagreements among us?*

- Everyone writes down the family challenge card on his or her *Soul Refresh* form.

- One family member prints on coloured paper with marking pens the blessings for the family and the challenge for the family and agrees to post it in a strategic area as a reminder for all the family members. See sample below:

> **Virtues for Family Harmony**
>
> Our Blessings: Acceptance and discipline
>
> Our Challenge: Forgiveness
>
> Signature of members
>
> Date Covered

- After a week the family meets again to assess the results of practising common family virtues, as well as individual virtues to create family harmony.

Section 3

3.3 Closing the Workshop *(30 minutes)*

3.3.1 Share Gains Made

Encourage all the participants to share their personal and family gains by asking, "What are you most happy about as a participant in the Family Harmony Workshop? Why? You can answer with a word or a statement to describe your positive feeling."

3.3.2 Get Feedback on Improving the Workshop

Ask for suggestions to improve the workshop.

Thank everyone for taking part and wish them all the best for the future.

3.3.3 Do Commentary

Play soft, meditative music and just say a short reflection based on the gains shared by participants.

3.3.4 Share Light Meal

Each participating family brings a dish to be shared with all participants.

I AM A STAR OF VIRTUES...

○ Paste your photo on the centre of the star.

○ Write 5–10 positive qualities around the star (as rays of the star) that your family members have observed in you.

○ Post your STAR sheet in your home to remind you of your inner beauty.

SOUL REFRESH

For a week, notice the change in your life when you live by your positive qualities…

My Blessing:

My Support:

My Challenge:

Name:

Date covered:

VIRTUES FOR FAMILY HARMONY

(OF THE _____ FAMILY)

Our Blessings:

Our Challenge:

Signature of family members:

Date covered:

JEWELS FOR LIFE VIRTUE CARDS

Balance
You are in tune with yourself and with life, therefore you do the right things at the right time, making your life flow naturally and easily in the right direction.

Courage
You have the courage to be honest with yourself and keep your intentions pure. You are not afraid to step in new directions. You know that each step of courage brings a thousand-fold help from God.

Beauty
With the inner eye of understanding, you recognize the beauty of every soul and the magic of each moment. With an open mind and heart you sense perfection in all that is.

Determination
You have unshakeable faith in your purpose and trust in yourself. You do not allow any doubts to enter your mind and therefore you reach your goal..

Benevolence
Your heart is clean and pure, filled with only good wishes for all. This makes you a truly great soul, Your presence gives courage and hope to others.

Enthusiasm
Your attitude to life is fully positive. You value every moment as an opportunity to create and contribute to the world in the best way.

Caring
You are truly caring, giving comfort and hope to all those around you with your gentle words, your true smile, and your patient attitude

Faith
You have unshakeable faith in yourself, in God and in the drama of life. Your faith makes the impossible possible. Your determined faith moves God to co-operate with you and your victory is guaranteed.

Clarity
Your mind is like a clear sky, free from the clouds of wasteful thinking. You always see the bigger picture and quickly understand what is appropriate for the best result.

Flexibility
Your life is like a dance, constantly in a natural and harmonious flow. You are open to listen, open to learn and open to adapt yourself to whatever is needed at each moment.

Contentment
Contentment is the jewel of all virtues. You embrace life with acceptance, appreciating all things and all people as they are. You are at peace with yourself and at peace with life.

Forgiveness
Because you love truly, you can forgive and let go of the past completely. In this way all wounds are healed and new beginnings emerge and grow.

Freedom
You let go of the past and are fully present at each moment to experience the wonder of life. You do not hold on to anything. Therefore you are free.

Intuition
You go into silence and listen for answers. You connect and truth makes itself known to you.

Generosity
Your unlimited kindness that never stops giving, reveals your generosity. Your heart is merciful because God has filled it with love.

Lightness
You are light and free from thoughts of the past. You see life as a wonderful game to be cherished and enjoyed.

Gratitude
You recognize and truly appreciate the gifts that life offers you at every moment and your fortune multiplies with each step you take.

Love
Love is the foundation of life. You share the purest love with everyone through your pure heart. Such true love does not demand but liberates.

Happiness
Your happiness comes from sharing the best of yourself with others from your heart, selflessly and without expecting any return.

Optimism
You recognize the hidden benefit in everything. Wherever you are you fill the atmosphere with positive thoughts and good feelings for all.

Honesty
Being honest and true to yourself, you earn everyone's trust. You do not depend on other people's opinions and are not afraid to stand for truth.

Peace
Peace is your true nature and greatest strength. You protect your inner peace, your most valuable treasure, never allowing the turbulent outside world to disturb you.

Humility
Humility is greatness born from self-respect. You are aware of who you are, so you do not seek approval, name or fame. You are free.

Purity
Your heart is filled with kindness and respect for every living being. You keep the aim never to cause sorrow to anyone, including yourself.

Integrity
You love what is true and choose to live according to your highest principles. Your thoughts, words and actions are aligned so you are trusted.

Respect
You recognize that each human being is unique and appreciate the beauty that each one adds to life like flowers in a garden. Your respectful spirit creates harmony and beauty wherever you are.

Section 3

Royalty
Your royalty is seen in your unlimited vision and generous heart. You have deep love for humanity, seeing it as one big family, and have genuine concern that all should benefit.

Strength
You have great inner strength transforming mistakes into wisdom, fear into courage and defeat into victory. You live by the truth and stand by your values.

Self-respect
You have understood your value and you radiate confidence. You inspire others to be free from the constraints of false ego. You see the soul in each one and recognize your spiritual brother.

Tolerance
Your depth and maturity help you see beyond the surface the deeper significance of everything. By staying connected with your true nature of peace, you remain tolerant and content in all situations.

Silence
Silence is the language of the pure heart. It is the voice of God, the music of love. Your mental stillness opens the way to the light of God and the means to absorb ultimate love and strength.

Truth
Truth is the still water of your clean and honest mind seeing itself deeply reflected. You cannot deceive yourself and no one can make you accept lies. You remain truly happy.

Simplicity
You radiate inner beauty and contentment because you have the courage to let go of anything artificial and simply be yourself.

Wisdom
Your wisdom is revealed, not simply through words, but through your whole way of being. Everything you do is based on deep understanding so your very existence is of benefit to all.

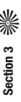

CLASSROOM

SHARING VALUES FOR A BETTER WORLD: CURRICULUM[1]

Introduction

The direction we take in life is a result of our values. The society we create jointly is based on the values of the people. This section offers a variety of ways for teachers to introduce and incorporate an exploration of values into the school day. Included in these creative and fun exercises are ways to investigate information about values and to use critical thinking skills to examine the consequences of particular values and their opposite for different members of society.

Target Audience: Students aged 8–14 years. Teachers, of course, will need to adapt the level of discussion to the age and interest of the students.

Duration: Teachers may wish to take up each value briefly, or they may wish to incorporate it into their curriculum for a couple weeks.

Objectives

For students to:

1) Think about different values and their effects;

2) Develop more understanding, motivation and responsibility in making positive choices.

Subject Matter: These lessons are an opportunity for students to examine values in relationship to themselves, others, society and the world. The values have been arranged to provide a sequentially based series of skills, which build upon each other.

---

1 Designed by Diane Tilman, an educational psychologist and author of the 'Living Values in Education' books.

The exercises include:

- self-esteem building skills;
- positive social communication skills;
- critical thinking skills, and
- artistic and dramatic expression.

Methodology: Exploration of each value can begin with the teacher asking the students what the word (that specific value) means to them, noting their responses on a board or flipchart. Then, the teacher or several students could read from Living Values their favourite parts of the Value Statement. Other statements could be collected from famous quotes collections. One activity or a variety of activities could follow to explore that value. Small groups, or the entire class, could discuss the effects of the value and its opposite quality. Plays, cooperative games and artistic expression of their output could follow. Ideas for possible activities are below. Teachers might also include values in the regular curriculum. History, social studies and literature easily lend themselves to an analysis of values as well as teaching at the fact and concept levels.

A unifying and summarising activity would be to make a large, leafless tree on a bulletin board with an oval, or egg-shaped seed below the trunk. The seed should be large enough to contain the names of at least 12 values (each to be written on a different colour paper). As the students work with each value, place the name of that value in the seed. As the students finish their unit on each value, individuals or small groups could write on leaves of the matching colour their conclusions about the effects of that value. Freedom could be green, with the students putting the fruits of freedom on green leaves. Respect might be blue. As the units continue, the tree – with its rainbow of coloured leaves – would develop, summarising the students' thoughts and providing a group memory and reference point.

A positive, encouraging, accepting attitude on the part of the teacher is critical to the process. Only with such an attitude will students really share what they believe and value and be open to the creativity inherent in higher levels of thinking.

1 FREEDOM

1.1 A group of students can take a powerful slice of its country's or the world's history and enact a dramatic scene related to freedom. (This can be done in conjunction with a relevant history lesson on slavery, independence, civil rights, etc.) After the skit, the class can participate in a discussion about what freedoms those people desired.

Questions which can be asked:

- Which of these freedoms do we have now?
- What other freedoms do we have?
- What freedoms do you think all people should have?

1.2 Ask students to choose their favourite famous saying about freedom. Have them stand in a circle and each powerfully state his or her one-line quote.

Ask: *How does that feel?*

Ask them each to repeat the root phrase, "*I feel lucky that I have the freedom to . . .*" and to add their own statement.

Or, they can complete the sentence, "*I wish all people had the freedom to . . .*"

1.3 Ask students to write a story on inner freedom.

1.4 Have students draw, sculpt, or do a 'living sculpture' of freedom.

2 PEACE

2.1 Lead the students in a visualisation exercise, asking them to imagine a peaceful world. Say:

In your imaginary airplane, you go into the future, to a world that is completely peaceful. What does it look like?

Imagine how you would feel as you step from your plane, how nature looks, what the air is like, how the houses look.

As you take a walk around a lake, let yourself feel how peaceful that place is, how you feel…

As you pass by a group of people, notice the expressions on their faces and how they relate to one another.

Ask the students to share their visualisations, stating elements pertinent to nature, the self and relationships.

2.2 Have small groups of students draw a large picture of a peaceful world together.

2.3 If the class were to make a time capsule to let future generations know about society as it was imagined in the visualisation exercise, what 10 items would the class choose to tell them about a peaceful world?

2.4 Ask students to write a short story about their most peaceful moments. *"I feel most peaceful when… "*

3 RESPECT

3.1 Explore the effects of respect and disrespect by giving half the class green armbands and the other half purple armbands. A 'pretend' government has declared the green group to be the elite. The government notices that the greens have a disrespectful attitude toward the purples. For a limited time period (perhaps one period in high school or half the day in elementary school), have the green group only give respect to other 'greens', while being disrespectful (in attitude, not words) to the 'purples'. Have the students reverse roles the next period. (The government has now changed hands and the purples are the elite.) Follow this with a class discussion on the students' feelings and perceptions.

How did they feel as the elite?

How did it feel to be part of the "un-elite"?

Would they like a world in which everyone has respect for all?

How would the world be different?

The day following the discussion, distribute a whole rainbow of coloured armbands. Now, they are all princes and princesses from different kingdoms! Ask the students to give regard to everyone through their looks, attitudes and behaviour. Discuss feelings and perceptions. Have them continue to wear the variety of armbands the next day. However, tell them that blue means they have the best education, green means they are hard workers, purple means they have a good sense of humour etc. End the activity with a discussion. What does this group (and all of humanity) have in common? *(All are human beings; each one has something to offer.)*

3.2 An enriching activity to explore self-respect is to have students explore their own qualities. Before this activity, the teacher may want to lead the students in brainstorming personal qualities, such as friendly, loyal, sweet, kind, compassionate and so on. Then, have each student write his or her name at the top of a piece of paper. As each piece of paper is passed from one student to the next, each writes the qualities s/he sees in the person whose name is at the top. Everyone's paper is passed to everyone else before being returned to the rightful owner.

4 LOVE

4.1 Play with combined words having to do with the heart – 'hard-hearted', 'soft-hearted', 'big-hearted', 'small-hearted', 'mean-hearted' and 'half-hearted'. Ask students to make a small storybook with an illustration of a different kind of heart on each page and a statement about what that heart would say. Perhaps they could end it with, *"When my heart is full of love, I feel . . . "*

4.2 Ask the class to imagine what the world would be like if everyone was loving. For a few minutes, ask them to visualise what a loving world would be like. How would nations get along? Say:

Picture leaders of different nations and how they would treat each other, picture friends playing, picture a family on a picnic and how family members would interact. Think about how you would feel inside.

After leading them through this visualisation, ask them to share. The teacher might want to do this with an entire class of younger students, or have small groups of older students share and report back to the larger class.

Another discussion question is, *"What wouldn't exist?"*

4.3 Have small groups of students make up a short sketch/play about a conflict relevant to them at school, or in the neighbourhood. Ask them to introduce a 'freeze-and-replay' element into the sketch, having the actors return to the actions and words in the play where the conflict started and where a loving attitude would affect the outcome.

5 HAPPINESS

5.1 Ask students to make a list of the things they like to do that make them happy. The teacher (in younger classes) or student facilitators of small groups (in older classes) might ask students to share in response to the following questions:

What kinds of things do you do alone that make you feel happy?

What kinds of things can you do with others?

Did anyone write down how they helped someone else?

5.2 Ask students to make a list of the things that others say that make them feel happy inside. 'Others' can include parents, friends, or teachers.

5.3 Ask students to make a list of things they can say to themselves that make them feel happy when:

- ○ Working on an assignment
- ○ Walking alone
- ○ Working with others co-operatively
- ○ Trying to understand something that is disappointing.

The class might discuss the self-talk or inner dialogue that everyone does and how we can use that to encourage or discourage ourselves. Have them share the items they wish to share in whatever grouping is most appropriate. When next working on a different subject assignment, the teacher might ask about their inner dialogue.

5.4 Draw happiness.

5.5 Play a game that everyone loves.

6 HONESTY

6.1 Have two groups of students make up a play, one portraying the theme of honesty and the other of dishonesty, or cheating. They might both use a common setting such as a stockbroker's office, a feudal lord of medieval times, a current conflict in the world, or a theme from a social studies unit. Afterwards, the class can discuss the effects, economically and socially. The actors can add how they felt subjectively.

6.2 Ask the class to write a short story using a real, or imaginary, situation in which a person lied. Examine how much energy it takes to cover the lie versus one minute of courage to tell the truth.

7 HUMILITY

7.1 Students and teachers could pick one of their favourite people, or characters, who have the balance of self-respect and humility. These could be famous historical figures, scientists, actors, or super heroes or heroines (Batman, Superman, Wonder Woman). Ask students to think of a few things that the character might say if asked what he or she were most proud of in life (or after a particular event). Have students pair up with a partner, pretend they are that character and relate what they are proud of with confidence, yet humility. Perhaps a couple of students could illustrate for the whole class. They might want to demonstrate a bragging tone first, followed by the quiet confidence and easiness of humility. Students could share their reactions to both.

7.2 Ask students to do something nice for someone at home, or at school, but with the feeling of wanting to help without needing praise. Was it hard, or easy?

7.3 Ask students to think of two things of which they are proud. Have them share that in a group of four people while the three listeners practise feeling the balance of self-respect and humility and offer positive remarks to the speaker, such as "Yeah, that's great how you did that!" Ask whether it was hard to resist trying to top the story.

8 RESPONSIBILITY

8.1 Have the class embark on a trust walk. Half the class wears blindfolds and a partner is responsible for carefully leading his, or her, blindfolded partner around, guiding physically as well as offering verbal information to manage uneven areas and to help the partner feel comfortable. Have them reverse roles later. Discuss the feelings of each role. How would you have felt if your partner were not responsible?

8.2 Have the students discuss the following questions:

What responsibilities do I have to the self?

What responsibilities do I have as a student? How do I feel when I fulfil those resonsibilities? (Older groups of students might discuss the long-term results of: How do I feel and what are the consequences when I don't meet my responsibilities?)

What responsibilities do I have to my mother and/or father?

How do I feel when people do not fulfil what they said they would do?

What responsibilities do I have as a person, to others, to society?

What would I like everyone to be responsible for?

Section 3

Students might break into small groups, with each group reporting back to the larger class. Older groups are likely to take longer discussion time. The discussion could be done in 15 or 20-minute segments over a few days.

9 SIMPLICITY

9.1 Explore works of art, historical pictures, or magazines for examples of simplicity versus something gaudily or excessively adorned. Make a collage.

9.2 Look at simplicity in the lives of your country's native peoples. For example, the Native American Indian tribes, the Adiwasis of India, or the Aborigines of Australia are simple, economical and wise in their use of plants and natural resources.

9.3 Take a walk in a nearby park, or go on a field trip to a botanical garden, or the seashore. Observe the simple things: the light on a leaf, a tree, a small flower, a bird, or whatever element of nature you wish. For a few minutes, simply be in the space of an observer, free from desires.

9.4 Draw simplicity.

9.5 Can you think of ways we can conserve in the classroom?

10 TOLERANCE

10.1 Ask the students about the lack of tolerance of differences they have noticed at school or in society. *Are some people tolerated less than others? If someone were really popular, would people be more likely to tolerate that person? What kinds of things can we say to ourselves so we can have more tolerance of others?*

10.2 In a history, social studies, or literature unit, ask students to identify a character who is different to them. To develop understanding, ask them to write a short story as if they were that person, explaining the beliefs and reasons behind the character's actions.

10.3 Pair up students with someone with whom they do not usually work. Have them interview each other. Have two pairs group up, each student taking a turn pretending to be his or her partner, telling the others about 'the self' and answering questions.

10.4 Ask the students to state prejudiced or mean things they have heard and quickly list those on a poster board or the blackboard. Then, ask the students to generate remarks that could be said in response – remarks that offer a more tolerant view but yet are assertive and 'cool' (neither aggressive nor wishy-washy). Examples are: *"Yes, it wouldn't be such a great world if we were all clones." "What would you do if you were in her place?"* Ask a couple of volunteers to model the responses. Lead the applause.

11 CO-OPERATION

11.1 Give one yardstick, or meter stick, to each group of five children. Ask them to measure the length of the playground accurately and quickly, using a team method. Give the teams 5 minutes to discuss their approach and then the game is on! Later, the class might discuss what types of things helped and what hindered the team effort.

11.2 Discuss the concept of 'true' co-operation as co-operation given with affection. Perhaps a group of students would like to develop a sketch about 'pretend' co-operation versus 'true' co-operation.

11.3 Apply the principles of true co-operation to a project that the class would like to do.

11.4 Divide the class into three groups and ask them to demonstrate the spirit of co-operation through dance. Have them select their own music.

12 UNITY

12.1 Enjoy learning about animals that exemplify unity, such as dolphins and elephants (the adults gather in a circle with their young inside when there is danger). Find stories of unity, such as 'The Lion and the Bulls' of Aesop's Fables.

12.2 Together, decide on a class or school project that will bring everyone closer to the way they would like things to be.

12.3 For the school's next International Day, or Peace Day, prepare several songs about unity.

Appendix 1

MAKING THE IMPOSSIBLE POSSIBLE[1]

The benefits of Raja Yoga Meditation

Politicians, scientists and other authorities are powerless to change this crumbling world; they can warn us about imminent disaster if we do not change our ways; they can cajole or inspire but they cannot make us reduce our carbon footprint and consumption of natural resources. We will change either because we want to or through force of circumstances (like natural disasters, war or a shortage of resources).

In India, monkeys are caught by putting nuts in a glass jar. A monkey sees the nuts, puts its hand in the jar, grabs the nuts and then finds it cannot remove its hand without letting go of the nuts. It gets caught because it does not want to let go of the nuts.

As human beings, we will only change our current destructive patterns of behaviour when:

○ We find something better to satisfy our needs for love, peace, security and happiness;

○ We feel at one with ourself and other human beings regardless of race, culture, religion and nationality and see everyone as brothers and sisters rather than competitors and/or enemies;

○ We develop a deep natural love for nature and see all animals as our friends with the same right to life as ourselves.

The impossible can become possible. But how?

---

1 Written by Margaret Barron, personal development trainer, and John McConnel, stress management consultant. Both are London-based.

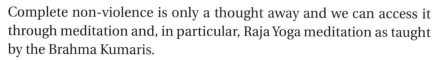
Complete non-violence is only a thought away and we can access it through meditation and, in particular, Raja Yoga meditation as taught by the Brahma Kumaris.

Raja Yoga Meditation is:

○ Consciously taking time to reflect on myself and my inner qualities.

○ Seeing myself in my fullest potential – full of goodness and learning how to express this goodness in life so that I continually bring benefit to myself and others.

○ Tuning myself to the vibrations of the Supreme Being, the source of all goodness – peace, pure love, wisdom and bliss. By opening my heart I am able to receive these highest vibrations and spread them throughout the world.

○ Holding a beautiful vision of our world even though it may seem far from it at the current time. This vision of beauty, peace and love enables me to perform the actions to help create such a reality.

○ Recognising that beneath the surface we are all spiritual beings, that we belong to one family, all are my brothers and sisters.

○ Realising that peace and non-violence is our original and natural state and that we can never be happy until we return to that way of being.

○ Remembering always, 'Om shanti' – I am a peaceful soul.

Practising Meditation: a Reflection

Sit quietly by yourself in a peaceful place , take a few deep, slow gentle breathes and read through the following reflection slowly.

I draw a circle around myself. On the outside of the circle I put all the aspects that make up my life – job, career, family and friends, house, car, everyday activities, hobbies. I let them all just be as they are. So often I am only connected with the thought process of the external dimension and unaware of the beauty that is within.

I bring my attention within the circle, which represents my inner world. This is the world of my thoughts and feelings, attitude, beliefs and perceptions. I begin to observe my thoughts and the space between my thoughts and notice how they naturally begin to slow down. I consciously allow the space between my thoughts to expand and fill my mind. In this space there is a natural stillness and quietness.

Consciously suspended in this space, I create one powerful thought "I am a peaceful being." I allow myself to experience deep feelings of peace and serenity. I begin to experience who I truly am – a subtle being of light that is totally aware of what is going on inside and outside of me; a tiny point of light energy that is the life force that animates this physical form and yet is separate from it.

Stabilised in this pure awareness of the self, I easily and naturally connect with the Highest One, the Supreme Being; a being of light like myself, yet eternally overflowing with peace, love and bliss. I enjoy these lovely vibrations and then find myself pulled into a dimension of total silence and peace.

I feel a deep sense of belonging, like a child meeting its long-lost parent. I feel safe, secure and totally accepted, valued and loved. It is as if time has stopped still and the only important thing is to receive as much love and power as I can.

Freed from all the trappings of the outer circle, I see everything with a different perspective – one of appreciation yet detachment. I am no longer bound by any negativity – I am still, free, powerful and full of love.

As I bring my awareness back to the physical realm, I am able to respond to the needs of everyday life with a sense of ease as I play my part in the world without being overly involved or distracted by it. I express my inner qualities and specialities freely knowing that simply by being in the awareness and experience of my true self, I have a profoundly positive effect on the atmosphere and others around me.

Having reconnected with my place of inner beauty and truth, I know that I can withdraw into it any time I choose because it is always within me; it has always been there and it will always be there.

The aim of my life is clear: it is not to take, search, or find but to be, connect and give.

Spend ten minutes in the morning and evening meditating in this way and you will really notice the difference in your life.

To find out more about raja yoga meditation contact your local Brahma Kumaris Centre. See Appendix 4 for further information or visit www.learntomeditateonline.org.

Appendix 2

10 WAYS TO CHANGE THE WORLD

The current distressing state of the world is the consequence of the past actions of humanity. Technical and political solutions to the challenges we now face are not enough.

There needs to be a radical change in the hearts and minds of people throughout the world – a realisation that the world will only change when we change the way we relate to ourselves, others and nature.

By changing our consciousness and reconnecting with our inner spirit, we will naturally and spontaneously want to make the world a cleaner, healthier, safer and more beautiful place, in which human beings and other creatures, can live together in peace and harmony.

Here are ten poerfulways in which you can help change the world:

Live Simply

When we use our mental, emotional and physical resources wisely and carefully, based on our needs rather than our desires, we are able to fulfil our responsibility as trustees of the earth.

Be Unlimited

By connecting with our spiritual essence and going beyond the artificial divisions of gender, race, culture and religion, we feel part of a global family and act accordingly.

Open the Heart

Practising compassion, forgiveness and unconditional love for the self and others, enables us to heal this shattered world.

Clean Your Mind

Putting a full stop to negative and wasteful thinking and using the power of the mind in a positive way is the foundation for world transformation.

Respect Life

Recognising the uniqueness, wonder and beauty of our own being enables us to treat ourselves, animals and nature with consideration and care.

Walk the Talk

When we remain true to our inner values and follow our conscience, despite resistance from others, our actions bring benefit to many.

Empower Yourself

Realising that we are the creators of our own world, and that we always have a choice as to how we deal with the challenges of life, brings a sense of freedom and responsibility, which gives us the faith and courage to make a difference.

Eat Well

Pure vegetarian food, cooked with love, nourishes our whole being and contributes greatly to the health of the planet.

Follow Your Dream

The more powerful, positive and detailed our vision of the future, the more likely we are to achieve it.

Feed the Soul

Spending time in meditation, or contemplation, gives us the inner strength and wisdom to deal with life in a more positive and peaceful way.

Appendix 3

About the Brahma Kumaris

The Brahma Kumaris is a network of organisations in over 100 countries, with its spiritual headquarters in Mt Abu, India. The University works at all levels of society for positive change.

Acknowledging the intrinsic worth and goodness of the inner self, the University teaches a practical method of meditation that helps people to cultivate their inner strengths and values.

The University also offers courses and seminars in such topics as positive thinking, overcoming anger, stress relief and self-esteem, encouraging spirituality in daily life. This spiritual approach is also brought into healthcare, social work, education, prisons and other community settings.

The University's Academy in Mount Abu, Rajasthan, India, offers individuals from all backgrounds a variety of life-long learning opportunities to help them recognise their inherent qualities and abilities in order to make the most of their lives.

All courses and activities are offered free of charge.

for more information : www.brahmakumaris.org
for Brahma Kumaris publications:www.inspiredstillness.com

Appendix 4

How and Where to Find Out More

SPIRITUAL HEADQUARTERS

PO Box No 2, Mount Abu 307501,
Rajasthan, India
Tel: (+91) 2974-238261 to 68
Fax: (+91) 2974-238883
E-mail: abu@bkivv.org

INTERNATIONAL CO-ORDINATING OFFICE & REGIONAL OFFICE FOR EUROPE AND THE MIDDLE EAST

Global Co-operation House,
65-69 Pound Lane,
London, NW10 2HH, UK
Tel: (+44) 20-8727-3350
Fax: (+44) 20-8727-3351
E-mail: london@brahmakumaris.org

REGIONAL OFFICES

AFRICA

Global Museum for a Better World, Maua Close,
off Parklands Road, Westlands
PO Box 123, Sarit Centre, Nairobi, Kenya
Tel: (+254) 20-374-3572
Fax: (+254) 20-374-3885
E-mail: nairobi@brahmakumaris.org

THE AMERICAS AND THE CARIBBEAN

Global Harmony House, 46 S. Middle Neck Road,
Great Neck, NY 11021, USA
Tel: (+1) 516-773-0971
Fax: (+1) 516-773-0976
E-mail: newyork@brahmakumaris.org

AUSTRALIA AND SOUTH EAST ASIA

181 First Ave, Five Dock,
Sydney, 2046
Australia
Tel: (+61) 2 9716-7066
E-mail: fivedock@au.brahmakumaris.org

RUSSIA, CIS AND THE BALTIC COUNTRIES

Brahma Kumaris World Spiritual University
2, Lobachika, Bldg. No. 2
Moscow – 107140
RUSSIA
Tel: (+7): +7499 2646276
Fax: (+7) 495-261-3224
E-mail: moscow@brahmakumaris.org

For publications visit
Website: www.inspiredstillness.com
E-mail: hello@inspiredstillness.com

Appendix 5

Further Reading

A Pocket Book On Virtues	Dadi Janki
Awaken Your Inner Wisdom	Sister Jayanti
Companion of God	Dadi Janki
Dare To Live	Miriam Subirana
Feeling Great	Dadi Janki
In the Light of Meditation	Mike George
Inside Out – a better way of living, learning & loving	Dadi Janki
Is There Another Way?	Dadi Janki
Living Values Activities for Children Ages 3-7	Diane Tillman
Living Values Activities for Children Ages 8-14	Diane Tillman
Living Values Activities for Young Adults	Diane Tillman
Living Values Educator Training Guide	Diane Tillman
Living Values Parent Groups: A Facilitator Guide	Diane Tillman
Practical Meditation	Sister Jayanti
Slaying the Three Dragons	Anthony Strano
Something Beyond Greatness	Judy Rodgers
Spirituality in Daily Life	Sister Jayanti
The 7 AHA!s of Highly Enlightened Souls	Mike George
The Call of Our Time	Dadi Janki
The Gift of Peace	Brahma Kumaris
The Heart of Well Being	Jan Alcoe

All the above books and a variety of meditation commentaries and music are available from:

Europe: www.bkpublications.com

Americas: www.bkwsu.com

Australia: www.brahmakumaris.com.au

Useful Websites

www.environment.brahmakumaris.org
A spiritual perspective on environmental issues

www.jankifoundation.org
The website of the Janki Foundation for Global Health Care – values-based care supporting practitioners and patients

www.just-a-minute.org
How to meditate when you haven't got time!

www.learntomeditateonline.org
A free 7 lesson course in Brahma Kumaris meditation

www.livingvalues.net
The website of the Association for Living Values Education International (ALIVE), a global endeavor to help students explore and develop positive values and move toward their potential.